Cow-Country Jargon and Sketches of Life Out West

Dan C. Cherrier and Dewey Colvin

Published by John Pulver, 2026.

Table of Contents

COW-COUNTRY JARGON

and Sketches of Life Out West

Collected by
Dan C. Cherrier and Dewey Colvin
Graduates of the School of
Western Experience

COW-COUNTRY JARGON and Sketches of Life Out West

2026 Anniversary Edition

Copyright © 2026 John Pulver

All rights reserved. No part of this publication may be reproduced, stored in a retrieval system, or transmitted, in any form or by any means, electronic, mechanical, photocopying, recording or otherwise without the prior permission of the publisher.

ISBN: 978-1-964094-07-6

Written by Dan C. Cherrier and Dewey Colvin

Notes for Anniversary Edition

Content warning: Some words included in the glossary are offensive, demeaning, trivializing and marginalizing. They have not been omitted due to their historical usage.

Text Alterations: There are occasional changes to the original text for spelling, grammar and punctuation to align them with styles more common today; however, many have been left unaltered in keeping with the vernacular specific to the cowboy culture of the time.

It is interesting to note how various words and phrases have filtered into common speech of today while others remain obscure and have not come into general usage.

Introduction

The West is glamorous. The almost Infinite space gives the newcomer a vision into something he can't understand. There is a distinct feeling of inferiority and then come the urge to see more of it. From the Canadian Line to the snaky, sandy bed of the Rio Grande, west to the sun-kissed coastline of the Pacific and east to the low-flung banks of the Mississippi is the Great West of our country. The West! Land of romance, adventure and—death! Breeder of stalwart men and women. Men and women who fought and bled for every inch of new territory conquered. To those hardy pioneers must go the credit of making our modern West possible.

In the West there is no room for small, petty things of life. Out here men are accepted for their demonstrated worth. The true Westerner has no time for crooks and pretenders. Your word is your bond. You must tally-up top-hand. You must show you're hard-up your back. You must have guts and wholesome respect for good women.

Down yonder in Oklahoma stands a silent, motionless woman. She seems to be staring into the vague, mysterious distances of the rolling plains. A wide-brimmed sombrero with turned-up rim brings her strong features into sharp relief. There is a neckerchief knotted about her throat. A belt filled with cartridges around her waist. She holds an old model rifle in her strong, capable hands.

The silent figure is that of Belle Starr—chiseled from stone. She was the first white woman in the turbulent Indian country. The statue stands in Ponca City.

The intent of the statue is not to keep alive the memory of Belle Starr—outlaw and desperado—but to keep alive the spirit and determination which demonstrated in pushing the frontiers ever Westward. Belle Starr, member and reputed ruler of the noted James gang, died with her boots on. Died from lead crashing into her soft body. Died as countless others of the adventurous brotherhood died. Each of those who stalked our frontiers contributed to the civilization to follow. The daring of Belle Starr, Wild Bill Hickok, Buffalo Bill Cody, Kit Carson, Lewis and Clark and John C. Fremont is still alive in our West.

The ranks of our oldtimers grows thinner. But let a new frontier open and equally fearless pioneers will step into the niche left vacant by the Grim Reaper. The recent colonization project in Alaska is an example of the willingness of Americans to combat nature in strange, new lands. The first call for volunteers brought an unexpected number of applications. These hardy pioneers are of the same calibre as Daniel Boone. Westerners all!

The West has proven to be a veritable gold mine to the writers of fiction. Members of the Inky Fraternity have endowed Western men and women with glamor, tinsel and artificiality. They have created a make-believe world in which swashbuckling *hombres* ride pell-mell, rescuing palpitating damsels from cattle rustlers, cold-eyed killers and renegade Mexicans and Indians. A question is often asked by readers who aren't familiar with Western fiction. "Why *is* Western fiction so popular?" To they who ask this question, all we can say is: Buy a magazine featuring red-blooded Western stories and see for yourselves. The answer lies between the covers.

The cowboy is a distinct type—courageous, reverent and a lover of the great outdoors. From his forefathers he has inherited a driving urge to travel; see what lies on strange ranges just beyond the horizon. See "how th' cow brutes 're doin' up no'th, down south or farther west." We are indebted to the roving cowpoke for the material in this book. Drifting from range to range, he took with him the terms, expressions and colloquialisms common in his home country and combined them with the new ones learned. In this way a new language has been formed. A language reeking with color and expressiveness—and one only native Westerners can fully understand.

Possessing lively imaginations and abilities to adapt themselves to any strange condition or situation, those and these untutored sons of the wide-open spaces quickly coined new words or twisted old ones to express their meanings. Where but in the West was ever a sleeper, a maverick, a never-sweat, a blind-bucker or a soogan ever found? Who could identify a hen-skin as a saddle blanket? A kak, tree or hull as a saddle? A broom-tail, fantail or a fuzzy as a horse? Who would say it is muddy enough to bog a snipe or muddy enough to bog a saddle blanket?—Only the Westerner.

The cowpoke has also drawn upon the Spanish lingo for words to identify many objects, such as aparejo, hombre, dinero, cavvy, remuda, bastos and barboguejo strings. The American Indian has also contributed to

Cow-Country Jargon. There is pow-wow, tepee, tomahawk, fire water, wigwam, make medicine, etc., etc.

We have no apologies to offer for Cow-Country Jargon. We have faithfully tried to set down on paper the quaint and colorful words used in the West. Out here in sunny California, where people are as thick as sand fleas along the Rio, we decided on this book as a means of breaking the loneliness of being on a strange, crowded range. Through it, we have lived again those happy, carefree days of our lives on the plains. In imagination, we have roamed the trails, peeped over the horizon and shagged windies from the canyons and coulees of our own—Cow Country.

Dan C. Cherrier.

Dewey Colvin.

Long Beach, California.

1936.

Cow-Country History
THE FIRST WESTERN COWBOYS

Down there in Texas, in the country lying between the lower Nueces and Rio Grande rivers, there once were extensive Mexican estancias. Thousands of wiry, half-wild longhorn cattle, descendants of those imported from Spain by the Spaniards, roamed the grassy pampas. Steeple-hatted vaqueros watched over the herds of wide-horned beasts. The estancias were large; covered vast areas of the mesquite and cat-claw blanketed hills and valleys.

And then came the Texas rebellion.

Back and forth across the billowing plains the Texans and Mexicans fought. As history tells, the hard-riding, deadly shooting Tejanos won out. Now only intermittent fighting was engaged in. Flying raids across the Rio by Mexican troops kept the frontier in turmoil. Lurking bands of Kiowas and Comanches raided the settlements. The Mexican estancias were deserted. The owners, to escape from the Texans and Indians, packed up, bag and baggage and hastened across the Rio. The wide-flung herds of longhorns were left to roam in wild freedom. The Indians and elements made away with the rambling adobe ranch houses.

The herds of cattle multiplied, became as shy as the antelope and brush deer. They swarmed over the valleys and lowlands; bunched on the uplands. And then down from the north came the sons of the men who had fought the Mexicans and raiding Indians to a standstill. Magnet-like, the strip of no-man's-land lying between the Nueces and the sandy Rio, drew the younkers. They were a hard-riding crew; dead shots with their long-barreled rifles. The thousands of roaming cattle caught their attention and with enthusiasm they proceeded to do something about the matter. Here were cattle; the gulf ports were potential markets. They would organize into bands and drive some of these Mexican longhorns to market!

The first band to organize was Cameron's. Forty of the young hellions flocked to Ewen Cameron for leadership. Ewen Cameron was a Scot. When he migrated from the rocky highlands of Scotland, he brought with him the native shrewdness of his people and the pleasant burr of their speech. Over six feet tall was the rugged Scot; strong as an ox and fearless. Ewen Cameron was a born leader, fair, square and resourceful.

These horsemen of the lower Nueces scorned the use of the reata—they ran the longhorns off their feet and corralled them. By the light of the moon, Cameron's Cowboys, as they were termed, relayed horses and chased the cattle. The wild, unrelenting chase broke the spirits of the longhorns and not too much difficulty was experienced in driving them to market.

Cameron's band of cowboys left a heritage when they passed on. They bequeathed a title—the Cowboy. Today, there are somewheres over thirty terms identifying the worker with cattle, but he is still a cowboy. (See *man* in the alphabetically arrange list of Western terms.)

Ewen Cameron took his band of sharpshooters into service against Mexican soldiers, and the licked 'em plenty. The rugged Scot was murdered while a prisoner of war, but his adventuresome spirit still lives in the heart of the men who have followed in his moccasin tracks.

COWBOY RIGGING

Each item of the cowboys' rigging serves a definite purpose. From his wide-brimmed sombrero to the thimble-heel boots on his feet, he is an example of efficiency.

His curl-brim sombrero shades his face and eyes from the sun wind and rain. It is also handy when you wish to water your cayuse. The brim pinched together also provides a cup for personal drinking purposes. Fifty dollars isn't an uncommon price for a high-grade sombrero.

The neckerchief protects the neck from the sun. The drag riders of a trail herd pulls the neckerchief up over the mouth and nose, thereby shutting out the clouds of swirling dust. In winter the neckerchief may also be tied down over the ears, protecting them from the cold.

The vest supplies numerous pockets for carrying small items, such as tobacco, papers and matches; pencil stubs, a "day" book and bachelor buttons.

The cowboy's "everyday" shirt is either a hickory, blue chambray and in winter, a wool one. Material difficult to tear is favored by all the 'punchers.

Levis or moleskin breeches are favored. The overalls are generally worn due to durability. The pockets, seam ends and other points of strain are secured with copper rivets. The genuine cowboy never wears bib overalls.

The high-topped boots, usually fourteen inches, protect the feet and legs from brush, cactus and cold. The high, slanting heels aids the cowboy in keeping his feet in the saddle stirrups while riding a bucking horse. The everyday work boots vary in price, and the fancy two or three colored boots, legs decorated with steer heads, stars and whatnots, sell for a much as sixty-five dollars per pair.

The spurs serves two purposes—ornamental and roweling a horse. Some sections prefer spurs with down-turned shanks; others prefer those with the shanks turned upward. The rowels vary in size and design. The Spanish spurs are heavy, long shanked, huge, roweled affairs and are stamped with all manner of designs. Prices of spurs range from a few dollars and up—mostly up. See *spurs* in the collection of Western terms.

The chaps or chaparejos are worn over the overalls when working on the range. Down in the Southwest, the 'punchers prefer the all-leather chaps, while in the north the riders go in for angora, bear or plain old goat skin chaps. A pair of angoras are extremely warm in cold weather, but have terrible odor when wet. Prices range from twenty dollars up, depending on the material and fancy doodads decorating them. See *chaps* in the list of Western terms.

The lasso, lariat or reata is a very necessary part of cowboy equipment. The material of the lariat is mostly hemp. Down there in Mexico they make a maguey rope which is a general favorite among cow folks. The maguey is a small, stiff rope but is extremely tough and isn't likely to kink. Rawhide is also used in the making of reatas. Hair ropes are greatly favored by Mexican vaqueros. Manila hemp also makes a good throwing rope and is light and strong. Lengths vary, and is mostly governed by the country. That is, whether mountainous, broken or plains. The usual length of a lariat is around forty feet. Some 'punchers are successful in handling a sixty-foot rope. See *lariat* in the list of Western terms for additional information.

The saddle is also considered on a utility basis. There are several popular "trees" advertised by saddle houses and each of them has their ardent followers. The 'tree' is the wooden skeleton of the saddle and must be of seasoned, tough wood. The tree should be a comfortable one to the rider as well as to the horse. The leather going into the saddle should be first-grade material. The saddle manufacturers build their saddles to order, thereby guaranteeing a fit to the rider. Saddles range in weight. The light, poorly built kak weights twenty-eight pounds and as the durability and price advances, the weight increases. Thirty-five pounds is the average weight of good saddles. Prices range from thirty-five dollars up. A good, reliable saddle sells from seventy-five dollars to one hundred and ten dollars. The full-stamped, silver ornamented, dyed saddles sell for a much as five hundred dollars. See *saddle* and *saddle tree* in list of Western terms.

Taps or tapaderos are the covering over the stirrups to protect the feet from the brush, cactus and weather. There are many designs of taps, depending on the rider's choice and personal ideas. They sell for as much as twenty-five dollars per pair. See *tapaderos* in list of Western terms.

Fence pliers and a leather scabbard for same are a part of every working cowboy's saddle equipment.

Saddle pockets, sometimes termed saddle bags, provide ample space for carrying dunnage. The pockets are double, and laced together. They are carried behind the cantle.

The bridle is selected according to durability and ornamentation. The reins and bits are purchased separately.

The bridle bits are a very necessary part of equipment. They enable the rider to control his mount and to subjugate the wild ones. There are numerous designs. The Spanish or spade bit is without doubt the most cruel instrument ever placed in a horse's mouth. See *spade bit* in list of Western terms.

Martingales and breast collars have uses besides ornamentation. See *martingale* and *breast strap* in list of Western terms.

The cowboy's horse is the four-footed friend of man. He must be wiry, possess endurance, be intelligent and active. There are many breeds of horses but the mustang has never been equaled. They are fiery, tough and fast; sometimes vicious and treacherous. Cross breeding of mustangs and leggy foreign horses has produced a type of horse found nowhere except in this country. The cowboy's horses run the gamut of colors. Separate the man and beast and both are helpless.

Only in the wildest sections do cowboys carry guns nowadays. Their favorite weapons are a forty-five calibre, double-action six-shooter and a rifle. They use the guns for killing predatory animals, such as mountain lions and wolves. Back in the dim past they carried guns for protection and punishment of rustlers.

When the cowpoke goes to town, he's an object of splendor. His work clothes have been laid aside and he trots forth in silk shirt, flowing neckerchief, his XXXX Beaver sombrero and new Levis. Forty a month and no board to pay. The outfit they sport usually represents a couple of years' pay.

And the cowpuncher doesn't wear suspenders—always a studded or plain belt. And he never stands erect when it is possible to hunker or lie down; never walks when he can ride.

JOHN SLAUGHTER
Rancher and Sheriff

"See that trail? Now you hit it quick and don't ever show your face in Arizona again or I'll kill you."

John Slaughter, black eyes glittering with death threat, seldom raised his voice when he delivered that ultimatum to countless desperadoes of Cochise County. One look into his determined eyes was sufficient proof that the little man meant just what he was saying and the bad *hombres* promptly followed his instructions.

Primarily, John Slaughter was a rancher, but when the fighting Earp brothers left Tombstone, he was drafted into service as sheriff of lawless Cochise County. Slightly over five feet in height, but possessing a driving will and grim determination, the little man shot peace and security into the wild country.

John Slaughter was born in the lowlands of Louisiana on October 2, 1841. He was just a lad when his family pushed westward. Westward to the Texas frontier. There the boy grew into manhood. When he was about eighteen years old, he joined the fighting Texas Rangers and aided in driving the savage Kiowa and Comanche Indians back into their territory across Red River. Even then, John Slaughter was demonstrating his utter fearlessness and a passionate love for peace. Peace at any price.

After leaving the service of the Rangers, he established a ranch known as the Atacasta. John Slaughter's slight figure was a familiar sight on the cattle trails as he led his herds to distant markets. He prospered. Then came marriage.

Viola Howell was the daughter of a prominent pioneer Texas family and a proper mate for John Slaughter.

1879. Texas was becoming too civilized for young Slaughter and his bride. That year he gathered his cattle, packed belongings into canvas-sheeted wagons and pushed into the hazy West. Twenty hard-riding Texas cowboys hustled the Slaughter longhorns across the dreary landscape. Over sun-blasted desert land, and forbidding raw mountains the cavalcade wound. The heat and privations were great but John Slaughter never faltered. He had his sights notched on Arizona and all the pitfalls of nature could not stop him.

There in the San Bernardino Valley John Slaughter established his bride in a hastily prepared dugout—a sod house. He then busied himself in carving out a ranch of eighty thousand acres, a portion lying below the border. John and Viola Slaughters' first child was born in that sod house. And then he built a rambling adobe ranch house. Cottonwood trees shaded it from the pitiless sun. Down in the valley along the Guadalupe and San Berdue rivers, JHS cattle grazed in sleek security. Little John Slaughter was on the highroad to wealth and prominence. He owned every foot of land his steers grazed over.

And then his herds were attacked by rustlers.

John Slaughter promptly buckled on his six-shooters and picked up the trail of one band of thieves. He tracked down his rustled stock and buffaloed the leader into leaving Arizona forever. Later, Slaughter was driving a herd through New Mexico and fate brought him and the rustler chief together. The meeting took place near John Chisum's Bosque Grande Rancho. John Slaughter killed Bill Gallagher with a rifle. Some oldtimers place the meeting between Slaughter and Gallagher to his move from Texas to Arizona, but the fact remains that Slaughter killed Gallagher, a noted killer.

1886. Tombstone was filled to overflowing with frontier riffraff. There was no law. The good citizens held a meeting and drafted John Slaughter into service. 1890 saw his work completed. The little sheriff, with his ready six-guns and blazing eyes, drove the lawless element from Cochise Country. While wearing his badge of authority, John Slaughter interpreted the law to fit the occasion, and he enforced it without fear or favor. There is no definite number of the men he killed. Only John Slaughter knew—and he took the knowledge with him when he passed on.

His task done to his own satisfaction, he then retired to his ranch in the San Bernardino Valley, where he devoted his remaining years of his life to his family and cattle raising. John Slaughter rode the range with his men and was one of them. He was fair, square, tolerant and termed himself "Just a cowman."

Then riding began to tire him. He contented himself in beautifying the ranch grounds. Far in the east the awesome peaks of the Dragoons pushed jagged heads into the sky and John Slaughter enjoyed watching the morning sun burst into molten splendor over them. The little man loved his valley.

February 15, 1922. The master of the San Bernardino retired early that night. He was eighty-two years old and not as strong as he had been. The next morning his family was grief stricken when they found him dead in bed. John Slaughter passed on while asleep. The ranch is still in the Slaughter family and is located eighteen miles west of Douglas.

John Slaughter sleeps but his handiwork goes on.

THE WILD BUNCH

Wild horses! Across the ridges, down the valleys they come, unshod, flinty feet drumming a thunder-roar above the swirling clouds of dust. There is the shrill whistle of the stallion, whinnying and coughing of the mares, plaintive cries of the shagged wobbly-legged colts. These are the descendants of the mighty horses the Conquistadores brought over from Spain. There's royal blood running though the fantails' veins, but one could hardly believe it.

The greater percent of the herds are runty, jug-headed, shaggy critters. Many of them are misshapen, deformed from generations or inbreeding. Not all of them were originally wild. Years back horse outfits let their stock run free on the ranges; many of them joined the Wild Bunch. Other horses strayed from the owners. And the stallions have tricks in coaxing mares to join the herd.

Ofttimes a cayuse carrying a warped, twisted saddle may be seen. The kak stays on the horse's back until the cincha falls apart or is broken. Many a cowpoke has lost a carelessly picketed horse. Perhaps the 'puncher was shot from ambush; perhaps the horse fell, stunning the rider. There are many "perhaps" to consider when viewing the Wild Bunch.

Even today there are thousands of the wild ones. It is estimated that there are 20,000 wild horses in Arizona alone. But each year sees their numbers diminishing. There are organized horse-hunts. Ranchers claim the bands of horses are driving the cattle and sheep from the ranges! Exterminate them! Ship their ganted bodies to the Pacific coast where they may be made into glue, dog food, fertilizer or canned and shipped to European countries for human consumption. Do away with the last representatives of our free and untamed West? Never! There should be an area set aside for these bands to roam upon. The buffalo, elk, reindeer and moose have protection. Why not the wild horses?

There is a two-fisted gent in Montana, "Powder River" Jack Lee, who is fostering a growing movement to protect the wild horses from extermination. Powder River is on the prod and a good and worthy cause. The treatment handed out to captured broomies has never been equaled in brutality.

A horse-drive is an extensive affair. First, corrals are built; then wings radiate fanwise from the trap. The riders take their stations, usually wiles distant, and sweep the uplands and lowlands free of the fear-crazed wild horses.

They are driven into the wings of the trap, forced ahead by riders on fresh horses. The cracking of guns, popping of rope ends, shrill yips and yells push the wild boys steadily forward. Eyes rolling, tongues lolling, they surge into the corrals. The drumming feet are dragging now, heads swing low and sides heave. Only the stronger horses have survived the grueling chase. Out there on the flats and uplands shaggy bodies dot the landscape. Now the coyotes and buzzards will glut themselves at the expense of the last representatives of the old West.

Desperately the trapped horses lunge against the restraining barriers of the corrals, seeking their accustomed freedom. Sometimes the bands are slaughtered there in the corrals. After the shooting is over, the carcasses are splashed with kerosine and burned. The organizers of the drives, who covet the few pieces of silver the horses may bring, drive the herds into railroad corrals. There they are starved and go without water, waiting for the train which is to transport them to the plants and factories. Bruised, battered, maimed and mutilated, the horses gnaw the corral railings to appease raging hunger. Water—there is none, usually.

There are laws protecting the shipment of sheep and cattle, says Powder River Jack Lee, so why not protection for the wild horses? Jack Lee is a determined man. He declares that the Congress of our United States is going to hear of this barbaric extermination. Oldtimers and other horse lovers are flocking to Lee's banners. They are riled good and plenty. Something is going to be done about this matter and be done *muy pronto*!

BOSQUE GRANDE RANCHO

1867! Across Texas from Denton County toward New Mexico Territory moved a vast heard of twenty thousand head of cattle, hundreds of half-wild saddle horses and a young army of hard-riding, hard-fighting Tejanos—Texas cowboys. John Chisum's outfit was on the trail!

A long string of canvas-covered wagons lurched and swayed ahead of the bawling cattle. Wagons carrying the possessions of John Chisum—the future owner of the greatest number of steers ever marked with a private brand. The Long Rail and Jingle-bob was Chisum's sign of ownership. The Long Rail ran from hip to shoulder of the critter and the Jingle-bob was an ear mark. There was no doubt as to the owner of the steer so marked.

When the entourage reached the Pecos River in far-west Texas, Chisum turned north, followed the river valley into New Mexico. A heavy cloud of billowing dust hung over the thousands of bobbing back and clashing horns. Bronzed, booted, cold-eyed Texans dashed recklessly about the mammoth herd of longhorns. Stragglers were choused into the herd; snapping reata ends and shrill yells urged them toward the horizon. Through wide belts of mesquite, screwbean, cactus and sage John Chisum led his men.

A large spring of pure, refreshing water was encountered in New Mexico and there John Chisum halted. There on a slight eminence he built his rambling adobe ranch house. It was one story high, thick walled and loopholed. The dozens of rooms provided warmth and shelter for the many men he employed. Later, cottonwood trees were brought from distant points by pack train and planted about the sprawled house. A double row shaded the long lane leading to the yard. Hundreds of acres of alfalfa were sowed; peach trees, pear trees and apple trees were packed in from far away Arkansas. The fast growing, luxuriant, climbing rose of Texas soon covered arbors, gateways and the greater part of the house.

This typical border-country home was presided over by capable Miss Sallie Chisum, daughter of John Chisum's brother, James. As a finishing touch in adding beauty to the Bosque Grande Rancho, Miss Sallie had her uncle import soft whistling quail and scarlet tanagers from Tennessee. Through the day and night their whistlings made life pleasant for the ranch dwellers. And then the lord of the Bosque Grande Rancho busied himself in cattle raising.

The ranges of Chisum's cattle stretched westward from the dreary Llano Estacado to the Rio Grande, and northward to the Canadian River. Fully half of the present state of New Mexico was over-run with Long Rail steers. There were dozens of far-flung line camps, each of them a miniature fort within itself.

There were Mescalero Apaches, cunning Kiowas and hard-riding Comanche Indians to fight. They resented the intrusion of the palefaces and raided Chisum's herds. They killed his riders whenever possible. John Chisum imported additional fighting men from Texas; men equally handy with a reata or a six-shooter. The boss of the Bosque Grande led his men against the marauding redskins. Within a year he had instilled a wholesome respect for his outfit in that wild and lawless country. The Indians and renegade whites avoided the Long Rail steers as if they were a pestilence. No longer did raiding bands of Mexicans dash across the border and play havoc with Chisum's cattle.

There were several million unbranded cattle running the West in those days. Mavericks they were and belonged to the man who slapped a brand upon their hides. Chisum branded thousands of them. His herds increased by leaps and bounds. But there were no extensive markets. Bosque Grande Rancho riders choused herds of steer westward to Santa Fe and Taos, southward to El Paso, to government reservations. But John Chisum saw additional markets far beyond the northern horizons. Markets which were to give him fabulous wealth.

The eastern markets had been brought to the West by means of the railroad, but the shipping points were hundreds of miles distant. There were Abilene, Caldwell and hell-roaring Dodge sprawled on the Kansas prairie beckoning with eager fingers. Cattle prices leaped from *one dollar* per head to *twenty dollars*. The West was rich!

Over the meandering Chisholm trail, the cloven hooves of countless herds raised a steady roar. John Chisum determined to take advantage of the rise in prices. Chisum was a shrewd business man. Here is what he did:

Taking between fifty and seventy-five of his riders, the boss of the Bosque Grande pushed into the rising sun. His riders roped and branded mavericks as the forged ahead. From the western boundary of Texas to where the Chisholm trail crossed the sandy bed of the Red River moved Chisum's growing herd.

There were thirty thousand longhorns carrying the Long Rail and Jingle-bob when John Chisum pointed northward up the trail toward the railheads. Across the Indian country the trail herd crawled. There were fights with rustlers, redskins and renegades. Lonely, unmarked graves dotted the course of the drive. After two months of fighting men, cattle and elements Chisum neared the long-sought markets. Cattle buyers greeted the lord of the Bosque Grande with open arms.

John Chisum sold his thirty thousand branded mavericks and cleared a half million dollars on the transaction! His riders raised merry hell in Dodge for a time and then followed their boss back to the New Mexico Territory. Markets sprang up everywhere. The forty or fifty thousand steers John Chisum sold annually from his wide-flung herds, were replaced my mavericks, bought herds and natural increase.

John Chisum was born in Tennessee in 1824, and when he was thirteen years old, the family trekked westward. Young John's father, Caliborne Chisum, started in the cattle business where the flourishing city, Paris, Texas, now stands. Fast ridding Comanches and Kiowas from the Indian country raided the frontier but Claiborne Chisum was a fighter. It was there on his father's ranch that young John received the training which later was to establish him as the cattle king of the world.

Young Chisum possessed business acumen and shrewdness far beyond his time. He could see into the future. There was nothing haphazard in the Chisum methods—they were a methodical people. When the elder Chisum passed on, John took the reins into his own capable hands. He added thousands of acres to the home ranch, and in 1854 launched the plan leading to his future greatness. Herds were driven east to Shreveport, New Orleans and shipped by boat to cities beyond his reach. But John Chisum had plans to carry out.

I was in 1857 that he sold his holdings and moved westward. He settled in Denton County, Texas. But civilization followed him and John Chisum wanted no part of it. Farther west was land to be had for the taking. John Chisum followed the driving urge in his mind. And then came 1867.

John Chisum never married; always declared himself as being too busy. He left his household management to his lovely niece, Miss Sally. His home was always open to anyone seeking food and shelter. The lord of the Bosque Grande

Rancho died in 1884 from Bright's disease, something even he couldn't combat. He was sixty years old when he crossed the great divide.

The Bosque Grande is no longer existant. Only crumbling walls and the stately cottonwoods mark the site of the rambling adobe house. Low whistling quail and flashing scarlet tanagers still haunt the streams and lowlands of the spot John Chisum called home. No doubt there are ghosts down there; ghosts of soldiers, statesmen, cowboys, gunfighters, outlaws and rustlers. There was a steady stream of callers at the Bosque Grande Rancho—John Chisum's feudal empire.

PLANT LIFE AND TREES OF THE GREAT WEST

arrowweed: A straight growing cane-like plant. Grows to a height of ten feet and is found in damp canyons and around waterholes of the open desert country.

barrel cactus: Biznaga; bisnaga. A large, cylindrical, ridged cactus covered with countless hooked thorns. Termed the water carrier of the desert. When the top of the barrel-shaped plant is removed and the inside pounded to a pulp, a viscid liquid gathers which quenches the thirst fo a certain extent.

box elder: A small tree growing along streams of the West.

bottle plant: Also termed Desert Trumpet. Found around waterholes and in damp canyons of the desert country.

blackjack: scrub oak. A stunted, twisted member of the oak family. Grows extensively in the Southwest, particularly in Oklahoma. Limbs are stiff, twisted and extremely tough.

burro weed: A species of plant life found in the desert. Burros practically subsist on the nutritious growth.

candlewood: Ocotillo. The Spanish lingo terms it *vela de lena*. This is a tree-like growth of cactus, but having no leaves and the branches are sheathed in thorns. Grows up to six and eight feet in height. This is a desert plant and gives forth a brilliant light when burning.

cat-claw: A tree-like cactus often mistaken for mesquite trees. Grows on desert hillsides and is covered with thousands of needle-shaped thorns. Mexicans term in *Uña de Gato*.

cedar: Grows high on mountainsides. The trees seldom reach a high growth. This specimen of tree life is found everywhere in the West but is seldom seen in the arid sections of the Southwest.

chaparral: A stiff-limbed brushy growth covering the Southwest. It is similar to greasewood or creosote bush. It is excellent for campfires.

cholla: Cactus. A thorned specimen of the Southwest desert country. Grows to a height of six feet.

cottonwood: A tall, stately tree of the West. It is usually found along streams and in damp places. The bark is gray, leaves triangular and bright green. Seeds of this tree are carried in downy particles which the slightest breeze will transport long distances. Grow high and furnishes excellent shade. Found everywhere in the West.

deerhorn cactus: A branched, tree-like cactus found in the desert. Branches are bare of leaves and are jointed. When the joints die, they fall to the ground and trap the unwary. The thorns are barbed and difficult to remove. Unfortunate is the horse of steer having a joint of the deerhorn cactus stuck fast to its nose. Each move only imbeds the barbs more deeply and prevents feeding.

desert holly: A shrubby plant of the desert. Rarely grow over two feet high.

desert lily: A true lily found around waterholes in arid areas.

dogwood: A small tree growing along streams of the West.

evening primrose: A lovely desert flower. Opens in evening and closes before the sun becomes hot. A favorite lurking place of desert rattlesnakes—the sidewinders.

fan palm: A true palm tree. Reaches a height of seventy feet. Found extensively in California arid sections.

fiddlehead: A hairy, slender-stemmed plant of the desert. Very common. Spanish: *Zacate Gorgo*.

greasewood: Creosote bush. Green-bronze in coloring. Grows in clumps and thickets. Found everywhere in Southwest. The creosote bush burns with a fierce intensity.

ironwood: A trim, well-formed tree found in the arid Southwest. Reaches a height of twenty feet. Twigs are stiff and thorn-like. Wood is extremely heavy and tough. When polished is ebon in color.

jack oak: Same as *blackjack*.

jimson weed: A rank-growing weed found everywhere in West.

Joshua tree: The yucca palm. Reaches height of thirty feet. Grows into weird, twisted figures. Found only in arid sections.

juniper: A cedar-like tree growing on the uplands. Juniper berries are gray when ripe. They rank high in medicinal qualities.

manzanita: A low-growing bush of the West. Found on hillsides and in canyons. Bark is crimson in color; leaves are small and oval in shape. Branches are stiff and very crooked.

mesquite: Mesquit. Spanish: *Mezquit.* A stiff-limbed tree reaching a height of twenty feet. Leaves are narrow and long. Grows singly and in thickets all over Southwest.

pepper tree: A native of South America. The height is great and the shade dense. Tiny red berries give the tree its name. No grass will grow under the pepper tree.

pincushion: Strawberry or fish-hook cactus. Seldom grows over two inches high. Is highly regard as food by desert Indians and Mexicans alike. Spanish: *Chilito.*

prickly pear: Pancake cactus. The flat, oval-shaped arms growing from the main stem are covered with tiny clusters of hair-sized thorns. Found extensively over West and Southwest. Also termed Indian Fig. The Spanish name is *nopal.*

quaking aspen: A small tree found along Western streams.

saguaro: Sahuaro. A giant species of cactus. Grows to a height of sixty feet. Trunk and body are massive and fluted. There are usually one or two branching arms near the top. The saguaro is a common sight on Arizona ranges.

salt bush: Shad scale. A species of plant life found in Southwest.

salt grass: Sand grass and basket grass. Found in damp spots in desert country. Utilized by desert Indians for food and basket making.

screwbean: A member of the mesquite family. Pods resembling huge screws grow in abundance on this arid-country tree. Desert Indians dry the seeds, pulverize them and after making a paste of the powder and water, thin layers are baked. The cakes are an excellent substitute for bread. Burros and cattle also relish the beans. Spanish term is *tornillo.*

smoke tree: Indigo bush. A small, desert tree growing up to fifteen feet high. Common along washes and arroyos of the desert. The branches are practically leafless and are gray in color. Viewed from a distance the thorned bush has the color of wood smoke, hence the name.

sotol: A species of cactus growing in arid sections. Mexicans brew a potent beverage similar to tequila from the fermented sap.

Spanish bayonet: Spanish dagger. The common yucca of the Pacific coast mountains and deserts. Early in the spring a stalk grows from the rosette of stiff, barbed blades. A lovely, waxen flower blooms at the tip of the stalk. Similar to candlebush. Spanish: *quijote.*

sumach: A small bush growing in the West. Late in the autumn the leaves turn a bright crimson. A cluster of berries grows from the tip of the main stalk. They are sour to the taste.

wild century plant: Maguey; mescal. A desert member of the cactus family. There are prickles on the edges of the stiff, narrow leaves with a thorn on the tip. Desert Indians prize baked maguey hearts, due to the heavy sugar content.

willow: The familiar willow is a common sight in any section of the West. Lines the banks of streams and damp spots.

white oak: A species of the oak family scattered widely over the West.

A MISREPRESENTED MAN

The following is a word for word statement of an old Texas cattleman regarding the virtues and sins of the American cowboy back in the 70's:

"The cowboy is the most thoroughly misunderstood man, outside of the localities where he is known, on the face of the Earth. I know him in all his alleged terrors, and as a class there are no nobler-hearted or honorable men in the world. Brave to rashness and generous to a fault, if you should be thrown among them, you will find them ever ready to share their last crust with you or lie down at night with you on the same blanket. Say that I have ten thousand cattle which I am about to send overland from Texas into Montana to fatten for the market. These cattle will be on the drive from the first of April until the middle of September. They are divided into three herds, with a dozen or sixteen men with each herd. I entrust these cattle into the hands of a gang of cowboys. For six months I know absolutely nothing of my stock. I trust their honesty to the extent of many thousands of dollars, without a contract, without a bond, with no earthly hold upon them, legally or morally, beyond the fact that I am paying them thirty-five or forty dollars a month to protect my interests. And these are the men pictured in the West as outcasts of civilization! I trust absolutely to their judgment in getting these cattle through a wild and unbroken country without loss or injury. I trust as absolutely to their bravery and endurance in the face of danger, for a man to be a cowboy must be a brave man. The cattle are as wild as deer naturally, and being in an unknown country are as nervous and timid as sheep. The slightest noise may startle them into a stampede. We have been on the drive all day, and night is coming on. It is cold and raining. We have reached the point where we intend to round-up for the night. The men commence to ride around the drove, singing, shouting, and whistling to encourage the animals by the sounds they are familiar with and to drown any noise of an unusual character which might provoke a stampede. Round and round the cattle they ride, until the whole drove is traveling in a circle. Slowly the cowboys close in on them, still shouting and singing, until finally the cattle become quiet, and after a time, lie down and commence chewing their cuds in apparent contentment. Still the vigilance of the men cannot be relaxed. At least half of them must continue riding about the resting herd all night.

A stampede of cattle is a terrible thing to the cowboys, and may be brought on by the most trivial cause. These wild cattle away from home are as variable as the wind, and when frightened are as irresistible as an avalanche. The slightest noise of an unusual nature, the barking of a coyote, the snap of a pistol, the crackling of a twig, will bring some wild-eyed steer to his feet in terror. Another instant and the whole drove are panting and bellowing in the wildest fear. They are ready to follow the lead of any animal that makes a break. Then the coolness and self possession of the cowboy are called into play. They still continue their wild gallop around the frightened drove, endeavoring to reassure them and get them quiet once more. Maybe they will succeed after an hour or two, and the animals will again be at rest. But the chances are that they cannot be quieted so easily. A break is made in some direction. Here comes the heroism of the cowboy. Those cattle are as blind and unreasoning in their flight as a pair of runaway horses. They know no danger but from behind, and if they did, could not stop for the surging sea of maddened animals in the rear.

A rocky gorge or deep-cut canyon may cause the loss of half their number. Those in the rear cannot see the danger, and the leaders cannot stop for those behind and are pushed on to their death. A precipice may lie in their way, over which they plunge to destruction. It matters not to the cowboy. If the stampede is made, the captain of the drove (trail boss) ride until they head it, and then endeavor to turn the animals in a circle once more. A hole in the ground, which catches a horse's foot, a stumble, and the hooves of three thousand cattle have trampled the semblance of humanity from him. He knows this. A gulch or gorge lies in their path. There is no escaping it. The is no turning to the right or the left, and in an instant horse and rider are at the bottom, buried under a thousand cattle. History records no instance of more unquestioning performance of duty in the presence of danger than is done by these men on every drive. Should the stampede be stopped, there is no rest for the drivers that night, but the utmost vigilance is required to prevent a recurrence of the break from the frightened cattle. This may happen hundreds of times on a single drive.

"I remember one instance which, from the friendship in which I held the victim, has made a lasting impression on me. Two brothers were together on the drive. Both men had been educated in an Eastern college, but for some reason had drifted to the cattle plains of Texas and had become cowboys. The elder was the captain of the drive. Sitting about the campfire one night the younger was very downhearted about something, and finally said: 'Charlie, let's throw-up this drive. I don't want to go; I feel that one or the other of us will never come back. I am ashamed of this but I cannot shake it off.' His brother was impressed by his seriousness, but could only say: 'George, here are three thousand cattle in my charge. I could not leave them if I knew that I would be killed tomorrow.'

"'A stampede!' cried one of the men. In an instant they were all at their animals, saddles were adjusted, and away they went. The captain gained the head of the drive, and had succeeded in turning them a little when his horse stumbled. In another instant, horse and rider could hardly have been distinguished from one another. This is the class of men cowboys are made of, and I never knew of many instances where they failed to do their duty.

"There is another interesting period in the life of the cowboy and that is the spring round-up. In the fall the cattle stray away, and in working away from the storms they sometimes get away a hundred miles or so. Each cattle-owner has his own particular brand on his cattle. The ranchmen in some natural division of the country will organize a grand round-up in the spring. The cowboys will drive the cattle together in one big drove. Then the captain of the round-up will direct the owner of ranch 'A' to cut out his cattle. One of A's most experience men will ride into the drive until he sights an animal with his brand on. Deftly he will drive the animal to the outer edge of the herd, and then with a quick dash, run the beast out away from the drove, and it is taken in charge by others of A's ranchmen, while the cutter goes back after another. After some fifteen or twenty minutes, A's cutter will be taken off and B's man given a chance. This will be continued until each ranch has its cattle cut out. If any cattle are found without a brand, they are killed for use of the men on the round-up. The cutting is a work requiring great skill and experience, and frequently requires the use of the lariat. Often cattle with a strange brand are found. If anyone recognizes the beast, a ranchman living nearest the owner takes charge of it and notifies the owner. If no one recognizes the brand, the captain of the round-up advertises it, and if no owner is found, it is sold at auction for the benefit of the Cattlemen's Association.

"These things will go to show the responsibilities resting upon these men. I will tell you how they get the reputation for recklessness. We will suppose these men have been on a drive for six months and been paid off. Then they are just like any other body of men; they go in for some fun, and on their lark ride yelling through the streets of some little town, shoot a few street lamps out or get into a saloon row. Now I know hundreds of cowboys who never carry a gun. They have strict ideas of honor, and they stand upon their honor. They are off duty, a lot of big-hearted, rough boys, but they are not outlaws or outcasts. They are not the class of men who rob trains or hold-up people crossing the plains, and I believe, taken for all in all, the American cowboy will compare favorably in morals and manners with any similar number of citizens, taken as a class."

PROFITS IN STOCK RAISING

Fabulous fortunes have been made in stock raising. It was the prospect of huge profits that made countless men trek into the West and venture even their lives in the big gamble. Hardships, dangers, privation and isolation meant nothing as long as there was the chance of making a speedy fortune. Those who aren't familiar with range cattle do not realize how rapidly they multiply. In the following table is shown the natural increase of one hundred cows over a period of ten years. A heifer should be two years old when bred. There is no exact scale to follow, but it is safe to say forty percent of calves will be heifers. The table follows:

100 cows in first year drop	40
100 cows in second year drop	40
140 cows in third year drop	56
180 cows in fourth year drop	72
236 cows in fifth year drop	94
308 cows in the sixth year drop	123
402 cows in the seventh year drop	161
525 cows in the eighth year drop	210
686 cows in ninth year drop	274
896 cows in tenth year drop	358

Total heifer calves born in ten years 1,428

SHEEP

The introduction of sheep into the West brought about bloody wars between the sheepmen and the cattlemen. The raisers of cattle claimed that sheep ruined the range by killing the grass roots and leaving their odor behind them as they grazed. The sheepmen retaliated by moving in more sheep; claimed that the West was a free country and open to any business. The resentment between the two factions flamed and then guns reared. There are hundreds of unmarked graves in the West; the last resting places of men killed in the fights. The wars raged from the sandy Rio to the Canadian border. Even today there is ill feeling between the ranchers and the sheepmen. In time the woolies were everywhere, gradually pushed cattle from the ranges.

It is claimed by many that raising sheep is more profitable than raising cattle, due to sheep being more fruitful in offspring, and requiring fewer men to care for them. Flocks of from one thousand to ten thousand are numerous. A flock, if properly attended, will double and treble in a marvelously short time, assuring the owner a handsome profit on his investment. Following are figures used as a basis for starting a sheep ranch back in the '80's:

Estimating that five thousand sheep are to be grazed, sufficient land for their accommodation will cost about $4,000. A flock of two thousand ewes, two to three years old, should cost in the neighborhood of $6,000. Sixty males, averaging $30 each would amount to $1,800. A team of sturdy mules and a saddle-horse cost approximately $275. It being necessary to have a working capital, a sum of say $1,925 is set aside. The total investment is about $14,000.

October is a good month to start in the sheep raising business, as the owner will have time to familiarize himself with his new undertaking before lambing time.

It is a safe estimate that seventy-five percent of the ewes will bear lambs, increasing the original band to three thousand-five hundred. One year from the date the rancher purchased his flock he may expect to have the following:

1,500 lambs (averaging one-half ewes, one-half wethers), a $2 each $3,000

In June he will shear his wool and get from:

2,000 ewes, 10,000 lbs. at 21 cents $2,100

60 bucks, totaling 1,000 lbs. at 15 cents $150

Income: $5,250

Losses; 4 percent on ewes, 5 percent on bucks $330

Depreciation $90

Expenses; herders, provisions, etc. $2, 223

Total Expenses: $2,643

Net profit first year $2,607

The years following should show a steady increase in the herd, and consequently a mounting yearly profit. The net year gains should run about one-third or thirty-three and one-third percent.

HOMESPUN REMEDIES

The gents, Alex. E. Sweet and J. Armoy Knox, tenderfeet from the East, took a trip through Texas back in the '80's and wrote a book of their experiences in that wild and wooly country. The entire account of the journey was written in a humorous vein and is a classic in its own right. The two explorers safely anchored their mustangs in a tiny village called Eagle Lake, and while there made the acquaintance of an old rancher whom they dubbed the Remnant. This Remnant gent, taking a fancy to the greeners, invited them out to his ranch. The following excerpt from *On a Mexican Mustang Through Texas* demonstrates the countless home remedies in use before physicians had appeared on the frontiers.

As we rode along, I noticed that The Remnant looked pale and sad. His solitary and pensive eye rested on the ground, as if it expected to find a lost dime. I asked him what was the matter.

"Oh, nothing! I'm just getting over the remedies," he responded.

"The remedies?"

"Yes, the remedies. I had a fever, and my friends have been trying to cure it. I got over the fever, but I'm still suffering from the remedies. My liver has lost all public spirit. It refuses to act. I believe the mucous membrane of my epide-gastrum is seriously compromised, and I fear peritonitis may ensue. It all comes from the remedies."

I may remark that The Remnant was much given to using words with the proper us of which he was not familiar.

"Well, tell us all about it."

I was taken with a violent pain."

"Where?"

"Just opposite the post-office, day before yesterday evening. I felt so bad I wanted to die, and be a cheruphim. It felt as if my spinal column was a ladder, and that there were five or six pains running up and down it. Just then Smith came along, and hit me on my shoulder until every bone in my body groaned, and asked me how long it was since I made my escape from the bone-yard. He told me that when I smiled it made him think of "Black Friday;" and he asked me as a personal favor not to do so again. Then he tried to turn it off by saying that Robinson Crusoe had a Black Friday. I told Smith my symptoms, after he had sobered down; and he gave me some good advice. Says he, 'It's all right; you've got it. It runs in families. It's the epizootic. All the mules in town had it last year. Go right home, bathe your feet in hot water, and go to bed.'"

"I went home in a hack, and described my symptoms to my wife's mother. She is a first-rate doctor,—knows all about herbs and other household remedies."

"What did she say you were suffering from?"

"She didn't make any regular Diogenes of the case; but she merely observed that it was a singular coincidence that I always had these spells whenever there was firewood to be chopped, and that they passed off about the time dinner was on the table. She hinted, that, if I would only pass off too, she would regard it in the light of a personal favor."

"If you can give me a lucid account of the symptoms, without bringing in your family pedigree, I would feel obliged. Try now, that's a good fellow!"

He assented, and gave me the following sickening details:—

"I put my feet in hot water, and boiled them until they seemed to be done; and then I took them out. My wife had heard that in such cases it was a good remedy to rub the throat with a piece of fat bacon sprinkled with pepper."

"Did you rub the inside of your throat with a piece of fat bacon, or only the outside?" I queried.

"The outside, of course. How could I rub the inside with a piece of fat bacon, when I had to gargle it with salt and water, and with borax and alum, every five minutes? All these remedies were bound to help me, one way or another. I didn't feel that pain in my back at all. I was so busy vomiting from the gargle, that it didn't bother me in the least. As I was beginning to get some good from the remedies, just to enjoy myself, a neighbor, who was a friend of the family, came in, and said there was no occasion for a man dying at all, if he would only rub the bridge of his nose and the soles of his feet with spirits of turpentine. I did not think he would lie about such a trivial matter, and I did as he said. I started out with a pain in my back; and, by the use of the remedies, in less than an hour I was suffering from a sore throat, headache, had four more red-hot pains running up and down my spinal column, and began to feel the symptoms of preliminary meningitis of the pericardium. Besides, I smelled as if I had been freshly painted. I had been plastered—mustard-plastered—already.

My throat felt as if there was a never ending torchlight procession going through it. Another friend of the family came in, and said there was no hope for my life unless a towel wrung out in ice-water was put around my neck. Somebody else had, in the meantime, prescribed castor oil and laudanum—as a remedy for the gargle, I suppose. The gargle was given to relieve me of the effects of the turpentine; and the mustard-plaster was to cure some Mustang Liniment that I was suffering from. I had a pain in my left side, but I didn't mention it; for, if I had, they would have shaved my head and put a fly-blister on it; and, to cure the fly-blister, some friend might have worked on me with a stomach pump. Some other benefactor would have given me a tablespoonful of ipecac, and sawed off my wooden leg. You see, I didn't want to feel too well: so I didn't let on about the pain in my side. That's what saved me from the remedies I didn't take. I took the castor oil and laudanum."

"Well, that out to have afforded you some relief, sooner or later."

"I went to sleep," resumed the relic; "but, just before I closed my eyes, my wife's mother greased my nose with a piece of mutton tallow,—to cure the castor oil, I suppose,—remarking, with her usual bland smile, that if death really loved a shining mark, that nose out to draw him. Anyhow, I slept. I dreamed I was making a speech from under a cross-beam, from which dangled garlands, or something of that kind. The sheriff seemed to be presiding officer. He was busy fixing the garland about my neck, and I was saying I could prove an alibi, when I awoke. My wife was taking off the wet towel. Mrs. Brown wrung out of boiling water what my neck really needed. They had the quilt all ready. The water was boiling. All I said was, 'Mr. Sheriff, do your duty. I want to die before another remedy gets here.'"

"How did the thing end?" I inquired.

"Well, it was pretty tough on a man with one leg in the grave already, wasn't it? But I got my six-shooter; and, laying it on the pillow, I told them I was going to die in peace. So I got well enough to be around, but I'm suffering yet"

THE COW-COUNTRY DANCE

The frontier dance is a looked-forward-to occasion. From distant ranches, line-camps, lonely bachelor cabins and nester shacks come the eager ones. Like the news Paul Revere spread the night of his famous ride, the news of a shindig or baile is passed around. Cowboys meeting out on the range pass the time of day and discuss the doin's over to the Bar X. Slowly but surely the news spreads over the rangeland. The Big Day arrives.

Cowboys have been known to ride forty miles to attend a dance! Forty miles across the grass-blanketed rangeland.

Rigged-out in their Sunday-go-to-meetin' duds, boots all shiny from liberal applications of grease or saddle soap, gaudy silk handkerchiefs snapping over their shoulders, brand-new Levis wrinkled into boot tops, the cowpunchers gallop in. A steady stream of buckboards, horses trotting and harness jangling come into sight. These carry the family men. Girls, riding spirited cayuses equally as well as the men, are in the procession.

The shindig is going to last all night. Horses are stripped of rigging, watered and turned into the corrals. Inside the house there is a hubbub. Women folks are scurrying about cooking. Out in the barns are hidden jugs of drinkin' likker for the men. Already, there is quite a gathering out there; a laughing, back-slapping group of clear-eyed, bronzed, lusty cow gents. These dances are few and far between and must be drained of all the pleasure possible.

The women folks are rigged-out in their finest and are in great demand. There is a dearth of the gentle sex out there in the wide rangeland and are object of awe and reverence to bashful young waddys. Considerable speculation, punctuated by sly peeping around corners and other safe points of vantage are engaged in by the youngsters. Countless romances have been started and ended at Western dances.

Come dark, the musicians, booted and spurred, tune-up their fiddles and guitars. And now the dance is on!

The exuberant yell: "Le's stampede!" is greeted with shrill yips and yippees. A buzz of voices; happy, care-free, fills the room. The Caller, a bearded gent, acting as Master of Ceremonies, stands near the musicians and his sing-song directions guide the dancers through the strenuous square-dance. His instructions invariably run as follows:

"Now fellers, shake your pen!
Lock horns to all them heifers an' rustle 'em like men;
Salute your lovely partners, now swing an' let 'em go;
Climb the grapevine around 'em; now all hands do-ce-do!
You maverick, join th' round-up, jus' skip th' waterfall
Swing your partners, wild, boys, an' promenade all!"

Square dances are not the only dances at a shindig. There are all of the waltzes, polkas and what-nots which the folks in the cities caper to.

And so on through the night. As the hours pass, the visits to the diminishing supply of liquor continues. Ofttimes fights break out. Old grudges are settled and fancied wrongs righted. If the host isn't a far-seeing gent and collect fire-arms as his guests arrive, there may be shooting. Usually there is a minimum of trouble. The more level-headed men quickly discourage any violent outbreak.

Back to the dance. If there aren't sufficient women to furnish partners for the men, which is usually the case, some of the men "wears th' heifer sign" which is a handkerchief tied around the arm. Great gravity and politeness is shown by the 'punchers begging the "heifer signers" for a dance. They are out for a good time and take their fun in a serious manner.

The square dance, sometimes termed a break-down, requires considerable endurance. The dancers are usually breathless when the fiddle squeaks a last strain and a last chord is thunked by the guitar. The music is in a class by itself. The tempo is fast and rollicking, and there is a quality in the melody which lingers in the memory. Favorite selections are "Buffalo Gal," "Dan Tucker," "Hell Among the Yearlings," "Turkey in the Straw," "Sally Goodin," "Fire on the Mountain" and for the waltz, there was never a more haunting melody than "Kelly Waltz."

The babies and youngsters are always corralled in an adjoining room. The mothers make flying visits during the intermissions to administer to their welfare. When the dance is well attended, there is sometimes confusion in cutting-out the numerous little Jimmys, Mary Anns, Buds and Johnnys to the proper parents. Sometimes young 'punchers, for sheer devilment, sort -of mix up the kids. And then there is trouble. Big trouble.

The oldsters, and they have to be plenty old not to take a part in the festivities, are always interested, critical observers of the dance. They gather in groups and discuss the prospects of the current calf crop, markets, grass and any newcomers in the territory. The older women visit with old acquaintances, follow the actions of the young men with suspicious stares and discuss the various happenings since their last meeting.

Dawn pushes aside the darkness. The dance breaks up. Horses are saddled, teams harnessed, kids packed away in the buckboards. And then the regretful parting. Another dance is planned; possibly three or four months in the future. Another ranch is selected; maybe twenty or thirty miles distant. And now comes the long rides to the various homes. The sun swings above the horizon. And now the reaction comes. Tired, sleepy, carrying pleasant memories, the dwellers of the rangeland scatter to the distant ranches, line-camps, nester homes and trading stations.

Life is resumed where it was dropped. There is hay to cut, fences to repair, wood must be hauled from the distant streams; a thousand and one duties to perform. But it is a pleasant, healthy life—Wasn't there another shindig just a few short months distant?

THE ROUND-UP

Open range is almost a thing of the past. Barbed wire and plows have done away with those vast sweeps of grazing land. But in the Southwest and extreme North there are still a few of the old ranges left. Nowadays, the cattle's feeding grounds are called pastures!

Back yonder in the past when round-up time came in the spring, ranchers met at a given point with their riders, cavvys and chuck wagons. They "threw-in together" and swept the range free of cattle. The greasy-sack outfits, usually consisting of three or four men, worked alongside the riders of the big spreads in gathering the scattered mammys and steers.

The selection of a round-up captain took only a short time. The man selected for that important place must be thoroughly familiar with the country to be covered and must know all the brands and owners in that area. He directed the search for the cattle and was in undisputed charge of the round-up. He selected the riders for the "outside circle" first. It was their duty to cover the territory lying the greatest distance from the center of the round-up. Other riders, covering the inner circle, followed the first groups to leave camp. In this way the circle was pretty well covered.

Within a few hours cattle came into sight, followed by perspiring, swearing cowpunchers. They had been routed from the uplands, the breaks and bottoms. Heads swinging, horns clashing, bawling and eyes rolling, the steers spread over the flat selected for holding them. Herd guards choused them together and as other bunches arrived threw them into the growing heard. A steady stream of cowboys galloped toward the chuck wagons. The grub wrangler, a flour sack apron tied around his middle, cussed as he dished out helpings of beans, Dutch oven bread, slabs of steak swimming in grease and gallons of Arbuckle—coffee to the uninitiated. Sometimes there were pies or apple sass for dessert. A cowboy never stands up when he can sit down, therefore they sprawled all around the wagons.

The 'punchers, mounted on the cutting horses, circle the herd, watching for the brand they represent. A pony darts into an opening, forces its way through the closely bunched critters and drives a cow with a bleating calf into the open. Individual groups form as the cutting out progresses. Fires spring up here and there. Branding irons, scoured free of rust and scale, and heated to the proper redness come into use. The cut-out calves are branded first. Riders rope them and drag them nearer the fire. The iron is pressed against the hip or side, ears are marked, and bawling, the calf breaks for its mammy. Maverick yearlings or full-grown steers are divided evenly among the outfits after all methods have failed to establish positive ownership of the critter. The tally man watches the count; knows exactly how many calves bearing his brand are running the range.

The work continues until all the calves have been marked with the sign of ownership. This is determined by brand of the calves' mothers. And then the camp is moved to a new scene, where the same process is repeated. At last, weary of the grueling hours in the saddle, a cavalcade strings out across the hills and valleys, heading for the home ranch and a bust-out in town. Forty a month and found—forty dollars a month wages and board—creates a hankerin' for the wild life of the cow towns.

When the fall round-up begins, the same process is gone through, only this time steers are branded instead of calves. They are cut from the herd, bunched, held into a growing beef herd and headed for the railroad. If the drive is to be a long one, a trail brand is stamped on the critters. As in the case of the Chisholm or Western Trails, the herds may be driven hundreds of miles across prairie and desert land. Hard-riding, hard-fighting and hard-playing cowboys drive the critters ahead. Back yonder in the old days, fights with renegade whites and bloody skirmishes with raiding bands of Indians were every day occurrences. There were hundreds of unmarked graves scattered along these two famous cattle trails.

John Chisum and his buckaroos drove one herd of thirty thousand wild longhorns, across western Texas, through Oklahoma and delivered them to cattle buyers in Hell-roaring Dodge. Chisum cleared over a half million dollars on the venture. (See Bosque Grande Rancho.)

Custom, climate and general conditions regulate the round-up in various sections. Only a general coverage has been shown here. Basically, these methods have been used in all sections since the first steer was branded.

MODERN-DAY RANCHES

The present-day ranches are something to make the oldtimer stare in goggle-eyed wonder. Instead of the sprawled ranch house, flanked by a bunkhouse and several corrals, there are slick lookin' bungalows all painted up like a Comanche on the war path. Instead of the good old kerosine lamps there are electric lights. Hot or cold water is available by simply turning a doodad. And there are bath tubs!

Back in the good old days the cow folks took a scrubbin' down in a wash tub or waited for warm weather an' jumped in the creek. And there are tales goin' around that cowpokes are wearing pajamas! Now when grandpaw choused steers for forty per and found, he slept with everything on but his boots and sombrero.

Nowadays it is a scandalous disgrace for owners to eat with their men. The bunkhouses are hid where society folks won't be pizened by associatin' wit the riders. (What few of 'em can ride.) There isn't a horsey smell about the whole lay-out. Even th' cattle have gone high-hat. Instead of havin' horns, the weak-stummicked critters are plumb baldheaded. Turn one of the pedigreed bulls loose to forage for himself and he's starve to death on a range of plenty.

And the cows!

They're somethin' to startle a self respecting cow feller! They don't resemble cows no more. They just look at you out their dumb eyes and beg for more scientific prepared ration. Back yonder in the past, cow brutes had fire and life in 'em. And the fellers what calls themselves cowpunchers have took up milkin'.

Now, when men were 'punchers and not farm hands, they wouldn't milk a cow for no man. They weren't calf-robbers. If they had milk they coaxed it out of tin cans. Barefoot coffee, that is, minus sugar and milk, did very well. When cowboys wanted coffee they wanted it black and strong.

And the offspring of modern ranchers!

Back yonder in the almost forgotten past, all the kids had a job to do on the ranch. These jobs made them healthy and self reliant; built strong men and fearless women. Nowadays as soon as the kids are dry behind their ears they are packed off to school, so maw and paw won't be bothered with them. After they are turned loose branded with an education, they return home wearing knee breeches and funny sox. The gals smoke cigarettes, play bridge, use paint like an Indian and gad bout in most nigh as few clothes as they wore when they were born.

A good old stock saddle isn't the correct thing when they go riding. They ride on those English kidney-pads. The boots they wear are a caution. Instead of thimble-heeled cow-country boots they wear those shiny, flat heeled English riding boots. Their mounts are usually of Arabian stock. Their ridin' duds are mostly hand tailored from material imported from across the big water. The Turkish tobacco in their quirlys smell to high heaven.

That stretch of prairie in front of the house (grandpaw took it away from the Indians back in the '70's) has been turned into a golf course. The way the kids can whack them balls with a club is something! They can drive one of 'em as far as grandpaw's old musket could fling a lead slug after a dodgin' redskin.

But,—and here is the only cow atmosphere of these new ranches—grandpaw can usually be found out in back somewheres hob-nobbin' with the farm hands, sniffing around the stables or settin' on a butte starin' sort-of dreamy-eyed into the dim past. Mebbe there's a lonely grave down on the flat where he spends hours every day, living again with his Martha the years of their youth on this changed outfit.

And then everybody, exceptin' grandpaw, packs up and lights-out on a trip abroad. As soon as the family is out of sight, grandpaw shucks his fyanacy duds and moves into the bunkhouse. Mebbe there's another oldtimer on the ranch, and the two old men may usually be found swappin' lies and squirtin' tobacco juice all over the yard.

Most all of the oldtimers agree that "the cow ranches tuhday 're jest sommers to make money tuh go sommers else."

TRADITIONAL COWBOY SONGS

The cowboys' lonely lives prompted meditation and pondering on the whys and wherefores of life. Out there on the wide, sweeping ranges, living close to nature, the cowboys came to wonder of the ranches up there in the sky. Such songs as "The Cowboy's Meditation" and "The Great Round-Up" resulted from their thoughts. During the night while riding guard on a herd of restless, spooky steers, he found that by singing he could quiet them. "The Dogie Song" and "Night Herding Song" are products of that discovery.

While following a trail herd on the move, the 'punchers whiled away the dragging hours by composing and singing such songs as "Whoopee Ti Yi Yo, Git Along Little Dogies" and "The Railroad Corral" and was pleased to find that his singing caused the steers to step more lively. In the bunkhouses at night they amused themselves and fellow 'punchers singing "The Old Chisholm Trail;" "The Dreary, Dreary Life;" "Texas Jack;" "Red River Valley," and countless other songs of the same type.

Close inspection and study will show that each of their songs tell a story, complete and finished. Everyday happenings in their lives provided material for new songs. Their pranks played on tenderfeet resulted in such songs as "The Zebra Dun" and "The Horse Wrangler."

Comedy, tragedy, sorrow, crime and bravery moved them to song. A leaning headboard on a lonely grave; a stampede; a train robbery; a noted gang of outlaws; a partner dying far from home and friends; the girl they left behind; a mother; darling sister. All these resulted in ballads of the plains. Some of the tunes are rollicking, fast moving. Others are of a sad and plaintive sweetness, haunting the memory.

Hundreds of the cowboys' colorful ballads have been preserved in book form. The composers' names, for the most part, are lost in the dim past. The material bodies of those booted bards have returned back to earth, but they left word pictures of life as they saw and lived it. Wherever the true Westerner goes he sings the songs he loves. Perhaps their voices are harsh and a bit unsteady, but there is a rampant spirit behind their words—the spirit of an unconquerable people.

"The Great Round-Up"

When I think of the last great round-up
On the eve of eternity's dawn,
I think of the past of the cowboys
Who have been with us here and are gone.
And I wonder if any will greet me
On the sands of the evergreen shore
With a hearty, "God bless you, old fellow,"
That I've met with so often before.
I think of the big-hearted fellows
Who will divide with you blanket and bread,
with a piece of stray beef well roasted,
and charge for it never a red.
I often look upward and wonder
If the green fields will seem half so fair,
If any the wrong trail have taken
And fail to "be in" over there.
For the trail that leads down to perdition
Is paved all the way with good deeds,
But in the great round-up of ages,
Dear boys, this won't answer your needs.
But the way to the green pastures, though narrow,
Leads straight to the home in the sky,
And Jesus will give you the passports
To the land of the sweet by and by.
For the Savior has taken the contract
To deliver all those who believe,
At the headquarters ranch of his Father,
In the great range where none can deceive.
The inspector will stand at the gateway
And the herd, one by one, will go by,—
The round-up by the Angels in judgment
Must pass 'neath his all-seeing eye.

No maverick or sick will be tallied
In the great book of life in his home,
For he knows all the brands and earmarks
That down through the ages have come.
But, along with the tailings and sleepers,
The strays must turn from the gate;
No road brand to gain them admission,
But the awful sad cry "too late."
Yet I trust in the last great round-up
When this rider shall cut the big herd,
That the cowboys shall be represented
In the earmark and brand of the Lord,
To be shipped to the bright, mystic regions
Over there in green pastures to lie,
And led by the crystal still waters
In that home of the sweet by and by.

"The Railroad Corral"

Oh we're up in the morning ere the breaking of day,
The chuck wagon's busy, the flapjacks in play;
The herd is astir o'er hillside and vale,
With the night riders rounding them into the trail,
Oh come take up your cinches, come shake out your reins;
Come wake up your old broncho and break for the plains;
Come roust out your steers from the long chaparral,
For the outfit is off to the railroad corral.
The sun circles upward; the steers as they plod
Are pounding to powder the hot prairie sod;
And it seems as th' dust makes you dizzy and sick
That we'll never reach noon and the cool, shady creek.
But ply up your kerchief and shake out your nag;
Come dry up your grumbles an' try not to lag;
Come with your steers from the long chaparral,
For we're far on the road to the railroad corral.
The afternoon shadows 're startin' to lean,
When the chuck wagon sticks in the marshy ravine;
The herd scatters farther than the vision can look,
For you can bet all true 'puncher will help out the cook.
Come snake out your rawhide and snake it up fair;
Come break your old broncho to take in his share;
Come from your steers in the long chaparral,
For 'tis all in the drive to the railroad corral.
But the longest of days must reach evening at last,
The hills all climbed, the creeks all passed;
The tired herd droops in the yellow light;
Let them loaf if they will, for the railroad's in sight.
So flap up your holster and snap up your belt,
And strap up your saddle whose flap you have felt;
Goodbye to the steers from the long chaparral,
For there's a town that' a trunk by the railroad corral.

"The Horse Wrangler"

I thought one spring just for fun
I'd see how cow-punching was done,
And when the round-ups had begun
I tackled the cattle-king.
Says he, "My foreman is in town,
He's at the Plaza and his name is Brown,
If you'll see him, he'll take you down."
Says I, "That's just the thing."
We started for the ranch next day;
Brown augered me most of th' way.
He said that cow-punching was nothing but play,
That is was no work at all,—
That all you had to do was ride,
And only drifting with the tide;
The son of a gun, oh, how he lied.
Don't you think he had his gall?
He put me in charge of a cavvyard,
And told me not to work too hard,
That all I had to do was guard
The horses from getting away;
I had one hundred and sixty head,
I sometimes wished that I was dead;
When one got away, Brown's head turned red,
And there was the devil pay.
Sometimes one would make a break,
Across th' prairie he would take,
As if running for a stake,—
It seemed to them but play;
Sometimes I could not head them at all,
Sometimes my horse would catch a fall
And I'd shoot on like a cannon ball
'Till the earth came in my way.

They saddled me up an old gray hack
With two set-fasts on his back,
They padded him down with a gunny sack
And used my bedding all.
When I got on he quit the ground,
Went up in the air and turned around,
And I came down and busted the ground,—
I got one hell of a fall.
They took me up and carried me in
And rubbed me down with an old stake pin.
"That's th' way they all begin;
You're doing well," says Brown.
"An' in the mornin' if you don't die,
I'll give you another horse to try."
"Oh, say, can't I walk?" says I.
Says he, "Yes, back to town."
I've traveled up and I've traveled down,
I've traveled this country round and round,
I've lived in city and I've lived in town,
But I've got this much to say:
Before you try cow-punching, kiss your wife.
Take a heavy insurance on your life.
Then cut your throat with a Barlow knife,—
For it's easier done that way.

“Cowboy Jack”

He was just a lonely cowboy
    With a heart so brave and true;
    And he learned to love a maiden
    With eyes of heaven's own blue.
    They had learned to love each other
    And had named their wedding day,
    When a quarrel came between them
    And Jack, he rode away.
    One night when work was finished,
    Just at the close of day.
    Someone said, "Sing a song, Jack,
    'Twill drive dull care away."
    When Jack began his singing,
    His mind it wandered back,
    For he sang of a maiden
    Who waited for her Jack.
    Jack left the camp next morning,
    Breathing his sweetheart's name;
    "I'll go and ask forgiveness
    For I know that I'm to blame."
    But when he reached the prairies,
    He found a newmade mound,
    And his friends they sadly told him
    They'd laid his loved one down.

"The Old Chisholm Trail"

Come along, boys and listen to my tale,
I'll tell you of my troubles on the old Chisholm Trail.
Coma ti yi youpy ya, youpy ya,
Coma ti yi youpy ya, youpy ya,

I started up the trail October 23rd,
I started up the trail with the 2U herd.
Oh, a ten dollar horse and forty dollar saddle,—
And I'm goin' to punching Texas cattle.
I woke up one morning on the old Chisholm trail,
Rope in my hand and cow by the tail.
I'm up in the morning before daylight
And afore I sleep the moon shines bright.
Old Ben Bolt was a blame good boss,
But he'd go to see the gals on a sore-backed hoss.
Old Ben Bolt was a fine old man
And you'd know there was whiskey wherever he'd land.
My hoss throwed me off at the creek called Mud,
My hoss throwed me off round the 2U herd.
Last time I seen him he was goin' across the level
A-kicking up his heels and a-running like the devil.
It's cloudy in the West, and a-looking like rain,
And my damned old slicker's in the wagon again.
Crippled my hoss, I don't know how,
Ropin at the horns of a 2U cow.
We hit Caldwell and we hit her on the fly,
We bedded down the cattle on the hill close by.
No chaps, no slicker, and it's pouring down rain,
And I swear, by God, I'll never night-herd again.
Feet in the stirrups and seat in the saddle,
I hung and rattled with them longhorn cattle.
Last night I was on guard and the leader broke the ranks,
I hit my horse down the shoulders and I spurred him in the flanks.

The wind commenced to blow, and the rain began to fall,
It looked, by grab, like we was goin' to lose 'em all.
I jumped in the saddle and grabbed holt the horn,
Best blamed cowpuncher ever was born.
I popped my feet in the stirrup and gave a little yell,
The tail cattle broke and the leaders went to hell.
I don't give a damn if they never do stop;
I'll ride as long as an eight day clock.
I herded and I hollered and I done very well,
Till the boss said, "Boys, just let 'em go to hell."
Stray in the herd and the boss said kill it,
So I shot him in the rump with the handle of the skillet.
Oh, it's bacon and beans most every day,—
I'd as soon be a-eatin' prairie hay.
We rounded 'em up and put 'em on the cars,
And that was the last of the old Two Bars.
I'm on my best hoss and I'm goin' at a run,
I'm the quickest shootin' cowboy that ever pulled a gun.
I went to the wagon to get my roll,
To come back to Texas, ded-burn my soul.
I went to the boss to draw my roll,
He had it figgered out I was nine dollars in the hole.
I'll sell my hoss just as soon as I can,
I won't punch cattle for no damned man.
Goin' back to town to draw my money,
Goin' back home to see my honey.
With my knees in the saddle and my seat in the sky,
I'll quit punching cows in the sweet by and by.

The words of this rollicking cowboy song paints a vivid word picture of the trail herd days. The composer of this song evidently experienced the hardships of the trail to Caldwell, Kansas, from the plains of Texas. The refrain given after the first verse is repeated after those following. The 'punchers making the drive to the railheads usually profanely vowed this trip to be the last. But within a few months they reappeared and firmly declared that *this* was the last trip over the Chisholm Trial, and on and on.

The original version of The Old Chisholm Trail could only be sung among men; rough men. Publication has toned this song down until it bears only a slight resemblance to the original.

“The Cowboy”

All day long on the prairies I ride,
Not even a dog to trot by my side;
My fire I kindle with chips gathered round,
My coffee I boil without being ground.
I wash in a pool and wipe on a sack;
I carry my wardrobe all on my back;
For want of an oven I cook bread in a pot,
And sleep on the ground for want of a cot.
My ceiling is the sky, my floor is the grass,
My music is the lowing of the herds as they pass;
My books are the brooks, my sermons the stones,
My parson is a wolf on his pulpit of bones.
And then if my cooking is not very complete
You can't blame me for wanting to eat.
But show me a man that sleeps more profound
Than the tired cowpoke who stretches his bones on the ground.
My books teach me ever consistence to prize,
My sermons, the small things I should not despise;
My parson remarks from his pulpit of bones
That fortune favors those who look out for their own.
And then between me and love lies a gulf very wide.
Some lucky fellow may call her his bride.
My friends gently hint I am coming to grief,
But men must make *dinero* and women have beef.
But cupid is always a friend to the bold,
And the best of his arrows are pointed with gold.
Society bans me so savage and dodge
That the Masons would ball me out of their lodge.
If I had hair on my chin, I might pass for the goat
That bore all the sins in ages remote;
But why it is I can never understand,
For each of the patriarchs owned a whoppin' big brand.

Abraham emigrated in search of a range,
And when water was scarce he wanted a change;
Old Isaac owned longhorns in charge of Esau,
And Jacob punched cows for his father-in-law.
He started in business way down at bed rock,
And quite cut a swipe in handling stock;
Then David turned from night herdin' to using a sling;
And, winnin' the battle, he became a great king.
Then the shepherds, while herdin' the woolies on a hill,
Got a message from Heaven of peace and good-will.

"Night-Herding Song"

Oh, slow up, dogies, quit your roving around,
You have wandered and tramped all over the ground;
Oh, graze along, dogies, an' feed kinda slow,
And don't forever be on the go,—
Oh, move slow dogies, move slow,
Hi-oo, hi-oo, oo-oo.
I hace circle-herded, trail-herded, night-herded and cross-herded, too,
But to keep you together, that's what I can't do;
My horse is leg weary and I'm awful tired,
But if I let you get away, I'm sure to get fired,—
Bunch up, little dogies, bunch up.
Hi-oo, hi-oo, oo-oo.
Oh say, little dogies, when you goin' to lay down
And quit this forever siftin' around?
My limbs are weary, my seat is sore;
Oh, lay down, dogies, like you've laid before,—
Lay down, little dogies, lay down.
Hi-oo, hi-oo, oo-oo.
Oh, lay still, dogies, since you have laid down,
Stretch away out on the big open ground;
Snore loud, little dogies, and drown the wild sound
That will all go away when the day rolls 'round,—
Lay still, little dogies, lay still.
Hi-oo, hi-oo, oo-oo.
——By Harry Stephens

"Whose Old Cow?"

'Twas the end of the round-up, th' last day of June,
Or maybe July, I don't remember,
Or it might have been August, 'twas some time ago,
Or perhaps 'twas the first of September.
Anyhow, 'twas the round-up we had at Mayou
On the Lightning Rod's range, near Cayo;
There were some twenty wagons, more or less, camped about
On the temporal in the cañon.
First night we'd no cattle, so we only stood guard
On the horses, somewhere near to hundred head;
So we side-lined and hoppled, we belled and we staked,
Loosed our hot-rolls and fell into bed.
Next morning 'bout day break we started our work,
Our horses, like 'possums, felt fine.
Each one "tendin' knittin'," none tryin' to shirk!
So th' round-up got on in good time.
Well, we worked for a week till th' country was clean
And the bosses said, "Now, boys, we'll stay here.
We'll carve and we'll trim 'em an' start out a herd
Up the trail east to old Abilene."
Next morning all was on herd, and but two with the cut,
And the boss on Piute, carvin; fine,
Till he rode down his horse and had to pull out,
And a new man went in to clean-up.
Well, after each outfit had worked on the band
There was only three head of them left;
When Big Add from L F D outfit rode in,—
A dictionary on earmarks and brands.
He cut the two head out, told where they belonged;
But when the last cow stood there alone
Add's eyes bulged as he didn't know just what to say,
'Ceptin', "Boss dere's somethin' here monstrous wrong!

"You folks smarter'n Add, and maybe I's wrong;
But here's six months wages dat I'll give
If anyone'll tell me when I reads dis mark
To who dis long-horned cow belong!
"Overslope in right ear an' de underbill,
Lef' ear smaller fork an' de undercrop,
Hole punched in center an' de jinglebob
Under half crop, an' de slash an' split.
"She's got O Block an' Lightnin' Rod,
Nine Forty-Six an' A Bar Eleven,
T Terrapin an' Ninety-Seven,
Rafter Cross an' de Double Prod.
"Half Circle A an' Diamond D,
Four Cross L an' Three P Z,
Bar N Cross an' A L C,
B W I Bar, X V V.
"So if none o' you 'punchers claims dis cow,
Mr. Stock 'Sociation needn't git 'larmed;
For one more brand more or less won't do no harm,
So old big man Add'l just brand her now.

"Dogies Song"

The cow-bosses are good hearted chunks,
Some short, some heavy, more long;
But don't matter what he looks like,
They all sing the same old song.
On the plains, in the mountains, in the valleys,
In the south where the days are long,
The bosses are different fellows;
Still they sing the same old song.
"Sift along boy, don't ride so slow;
Havn't go much time but a long ways to go.
Quirt him in the shoulders and rake him down the hip;
I've cut you toppy mounts, boys, now pair off and rip.
Bunch the heard at the old meet,
Then beat 'em on the tail;
Rake 'em up and down the sides
And hit the shortest trail."

"The Cowboy's Meditation"

At midnight when the cattle are sleeping
On my saddle I pillow my head,
And up at the heavens lie peeping
From out of my cold, grassy bed,—
Often and often I wondered
At night when lying alone
If every bright star up yonder
Is a big peopled world like our own.
Are they worlds with their ranges and ranches?
Do they ring with rough rider refrains?
Do the cowboys scrap there with the Comanches
And other Red Men of the plains?
Are the hills covered over with cattle
In those mystic worlds far, far away?
Do the ranch-houses ring with the prattle
Of sweet little children at play?
At night in the bright stars up yonder
Do the cowboys lie down to their rest?
Do they game at this old world and wonder
If rough riders dash over its breast?
Do they list to the wolves in the canyons?
Do they watch the night owl in its flight,
With their horse their only companion
While guarding the herd through the night?
Sometimes when a bright star is twinkling
Like a diamond set in the sky,
I find myself lying and thinking,
It may be God's heaven is nigh.
I wonder if there I shall meet her,
My mother whom God took away;
If in the star-heavens I'll greet her
At the round-up that's on the last day.

In the east the great daylight is breaking
And into my saddle I spring;
The cattle from sleep are awakening,
The heaven-thoughts from me take wing,
The eyes of my broncho are flashing,
Impatient he pulls at the reins,
And off round the herd I go dashing,
A reckless cowboy of the plains.

"A Home on the Range"

Oh, give me a home where the buffalo roam,
Where the deer and the antelope play,
Where seldom is heard a discouraging word
And the skies are not clouded all day.
Refrain.
Home, home on the range

Where the deer and the antelope play;
Where seldom is heard a discourage word
And the skies are not clouded all day.

Where the air is so pure, the zephyrs so free,
The breezes so balmy and bright,
That I would not exchange my home of the range
For all the cities so bright.
Refrain.
The red man was pressed from this part of the West,
He's likely no more to return
To the banks of the Red River where seldom if ever
Their flickering campfires to burn.
Refrain.
How often at night when the heavens are bright
With the light from the glittering stars,
Have I stood there amazed and asked as I gazed
If their glory exceeds that or ours.
Refrain.
Oh, I love these wild flowers in this dear land of ours,
The curlew I love to hear scream,
And I love the white rocks and the antelope flocks
That graze on the mountain tops green.
Refrain.
Oh, give me a land where the bright diamond sand

Flows leisurely down the stream;
Where the graceful white swan goes gliding along
Like a maid in a heavenly dream.
Refrain.
Then I would not exchange my home on the range,
Where the deer and the antelope play;
Where seldom is heard a discouraging word
And the skies are not clouded all day.
Refrain

“The Dreary, Dreary Life”

A cowboy's life is a dreary, dreary life;
Some say it's free from care;
Rounding-up the cattle from morning 'till night
In the middle of the prairie so bare.
Half past four, the noisy cook will roar
"Whoop a whoop a hey!"
Slowly you will rise with sleepy feeling eyes,
The sweet, dreamy night passed away.
The cowboy's life is a dreary, dreary life,
He's driven through heat or cold,
When the rich man's sleeping on his velvet couch,
Dreaming of his silver and gold.
Springtime sets in, double trouble will begin,
The weather is fierce and cold,
Clothes are wet and frozen to our necks,
The cattle we can scarcely hold.
The wolves and owls with their terrifying howls
Disturb us in our midnight dream,
As we lie on our slickers, on a cold, rainy night,
'Way over on the Pecos stream.
Talk about your farms and your city charms,
Talk about your silver and gold,
Take a cowboy's advice, get a rich and lovely wife,
And always, always stay at home.

“Red River Valley”

From this valley they say you are going
We will miss your bright eyes and sweet smile,
For they say you are taking the sunshine
That brightens our pathway awhile.
Refrain.
Come and sit by my side if you love me,
Do not hasten to bid me adieu,
But remember the Red River valley
And the girl that has loved you so true.
Won't you think of the valley you're leaving?
Oh, how lonely, how sad it will be,
Oh, think of the fond heart you're breaking,
And the grief you're causing me to see.
Refrain.
From this valley they say you are going,
When you go, may your darling go, too?
Would you leave her behind unprotected
When she loves no other but you?
Refrain.
As you go to your home by the ocean
May you never forget those sweet hours
That we spent in the Red River valley
And the love we exchanged 'mid the flowers.
Refrain.

"Whoopee Ti Yi Yo, Git Along Little Dogies"

As I walked out one morning for pleasure,
I spied a young cowpuncher all riding alone;
His hat was throwed back and his spurs was a jingling,
As he approached me s-singing this song.
Chorus:
Whoopee ti yi yo git along little dogies,
It's your misfortune, and none of my own.
Whoopee ti yi yo git along little dogies,
For you know Wyoming will be your new home.
Early in the spring we round-up the dogies,
Mark and brand and bob off their tails;
Round-up our horses, load up the chuck wagon,
Then throw the dogies upon the trail.
It's whooping and yelling and driving the dogies;
Oh, how I wish you would go on;
It's whooping and punching and go on little dogies,
For you know Wyoming will be your new home.
Some boys go up the trail for pleasure,
But that's where you get it most awfully wrong,—
For you havn't any idea the trouble they give us
While we go driving them all along.
When the night comes on and we hold them on the bed-ground,
These little dogies that roll on so slow;
Roll up the herd and cut out the strays,
And roll the little dogies that never rolled before.
Your mother she was raised 'way down in Texas,
Where the jimson weed and sand-burrs grow;
Now we'll fill you up on prickly pear and cholla
'till you're ready for the trail to Idaho.
Oh, you'll be soup for Uncle Sam's Injuns;
"It's beef, heap beef," I hear them cry.
Git along, git along, git along little dogies

You're going to be beef steers by and by.

"Texas Cowboy"

Oh, I'm a Texas cowboy,
Far away from home,
If I ever get back to Texas
I never more will roam.
Montana is too cold for me
And the winters are too long;
Before the round-ups do begin
Our money is all gone.
Take this old hen-skin bedding,
Too thin to keep me warm,—
I nearly froze to death, my boys,
Whenever there's a storm.
And take this old "tarpoleon,"
Too thin to shield my frame,—
I got it down in Nebraska
A-dealin' a Monte game.
Now to win these fancy leggings
I'll have enough to do;
They cost me twenty dollars
The day that they were new.
I have an outfit on the Mussel Shell,
But that I'll never see,
Unless I get to represent
The Circle or DT.
I've worked down in Nebraska
Where the grass grows ten feet high,
And the cattle are such rustlers
That they seldom ever die.
I've worked up in the sand hills
And down upon the Platte,
Where the cowboys are good fellows
And the cattle always fat.

I've traveled lots of country,—
Nebraska's hill of sand,
Down through the Indian Nation,
And up the Rio Grande.
But the Badlands of Montana
Are the worst I've ever seen,
The cowboys are all tenderfeet
And the dogies are too lean.
If you want to see some badlands,
Go over on the Dry;
You will bog down in the coulees
Where the mountains reach the sky.
A tenderfoot to lead you
Who never knows the way,
You are playing in the best of luck
If you eat more than once a day.
Your grub is bread and bacon
And coffee black as ink;
The water is so full of alkali
It is hardly fit to drink.
They will wake you in the morning
Before the break of day,
And send you on a circle
A hundred miles away.
All along the Yellowstone
'Tis cold the whole year round;
You will surely get consumption
By sleeping on the ground.
Work in Montana
is six months in the year;
When all your bills are settled
There is nothing left for beer.
Come all you Texas cowboys
And warning take from me,
And do not go to Montana

To spend your money free.
But stay at home in Texas
Where work lasts the year around,
And you will never catch consumption
By sleeping on the ground.

The words of this song illustrate the wanderings of the cowboys from their home ranges. That urge to see what lies just over the horizon sent them in all directions. The 'punchers drifting to new ranges is what made Cow Country Jargon possible. All the localities named in Texas Cowboy may be found on any good map of the United States.

"The Zebra Dun"

We were camped on the plains at the head of the Cimarron
When along came a stranger and stopped to arger some.
He looked so very foolish that we began to look around,
We thought he was a greenhorn that had just escaped from town.
We asked if he had been to breakfast; he hadn't had a smear,
So we opened up the chuck-box and bade him have his share.
He took a cup of coffee and some biscuits and some beans,
And then began to talk and tell about foreign kings and queens.
About the Spanish War and fighting on the seas
With guns as big as steers and ramrods big as trees,—
And about Paul Jones, a mean, fighting son of a gun.
Who was the grittiest cuss that ever pulled a gun.
Such an educated feller his thoughts just came in herds,
He astonished all them cowboys with them jaw-breaking words.
He just kept on talking till he made the boys all sick,
And they began to look around just how to play a trick.
He said he had lost his job up the Santa Fe
And was going across the plains to strike the 7-D.
He didn't say how come it, some trouble with the boss,
But said he'd like to borrow a nice fat saddle hoss.
That tickled all the boys to death, they laughed 'way down in their sleeves,—
"We will lend you a horse just as fresh and fat as you please."
Shorty grabbed a lariat and roped the Zebra Dun
And turned him over to the stranger and waited for the fun.
Old Dunny was a rocky outlaw that had grown so awful wild
That he could paw the white out of the moon every jump for a mile.
Old Dunny stood right still,—as if he didn't know,—
Until he was saddled and ready to go.
When the stranger hit the saddle, old Dunny quit the earth
And traveled right straight up for all that he was worth.
A-pitching and a-squealing, a-having well-eyed fits,

His hind feet perpendicular, his front ones on the bits.
We could see the tops of the mountains under Dunny every jump,
But the stranger he was growed there just like the camel's hump;
The stranger sat upon him and curled his black mustache
Just like a summer boarder waiting for his hash.
He thumped him in the shoulders and spurred him when he whirled,
To show them flunky 'punchers that he was the wolf of the world.
When the stranger had dismounted once more upon the ground,
We knew he was a thoroughbred and not a gent from town.
The boss who was standing round watching of the show,
Walked right up to the stranger and told him he needn't go,—
"If you can use the lasso like you rode old Zebra Dun,
You are the man I've been looking for since the year one."
Oh, he could twirl the lariat and he didn't do it slow,
He could catch them fore feet nine out of ten for any kind of dough.
And when the herd stampeded he was always on the spot
and set them to milling like the boiling of a pot.
There's one thing I've learned since I been born,
That every educated feller ain't a plumb greenhorn.

"A Cow Camp on the Range"

Oh, the prairie dogs are screaming,
And the birds are on the wing,
See the heel flies chase the heifer, boys!
'Tis the first class sign of spring.
The elm wood is budding,
The earth is turning green.
See the pretty things of nature
That make life a pleasant dream!
I'm just living through the winter
To enjoy the coming change,
For there is no place so homelike
As a cow camp on the range.
The boss is smiling radiant,
Radiant as the setting sun;
For he knows he's stealing glories,
For he ain't a-cussing none.
The cook is at the chuck-box
Whistling "Heifer in the Green,"
Making baking powder biscuits, boys,
While the pot is bilin' beans.
The boys untie their bedding
And unroll it on the run,
For they're in a monstrous hurry
For the supper's almost done.
"Here's your bloody wolf bait,"
Cried the cook's familiar voice
As he climbed the wagon wheel
To watch the cowboys all rejoice.
Then all thoughts were turned from reverence
To a plate of beef and beans,
As we graze on beef and biscuits
Like yearlings on the range.

To the dickens with your city
Where they herd the brainless brats,
On a range so badly crowded
There ain't room to cuss the cat.
This life is not so sumptuous,
I'm not longing for a change,
For there is no place so homelike
As a cow camp on the range.

COWBOY LINGO and PHRASES

If you can get ***the drop*** on a gent and make him ***stand hitched*** until you can pull ***his tail 'til he hollers what fur,*** you've done something. In plain talk this means if you can cover the gent *first* with your gun and make him stand still until you do whatever you intend to do, you've done something. To ***do a hoolihan*** is to turn a flip from a bucking horse's back. Gents who carry ***runnin' irons under their saddle skirts*** are fellers who'll bear watching. A feller that ***skinned out in a rush*** likely had the law after him and departed in a hurry.

In Texas, the term ***Texican cotton pickers*** are fightin' words. When a critter's ***too dead to skin,*** said animal is in an advanced state of decay. When a gent is referred to as being ***ring-tailed,*** he's plenty ***salty*** —that is, he's a bad man. When you can ***hang the deadwood*** on a feller, he's a ***gone goslin.*** Which means if you can prove anything for certain, the man's due for a hanging or a term in jail. ***A flash in the pan*** is something of no importance. When a ***button*** is said to be ***off the same bolt*** as his father, it means the lad resembles the old man in features, disposition and characteristics.

Anything ***all wool and a yard wide*** is the real stuff. When you say ***as sure as little green apples have specks on 'em,*** there's no doubt regarding the trueness of the assertion. If a feller ***puts his back up,*** he becomes angry. And when a gent leaves ***with his foot in his hand,*** he's going in a hurry. ***Bustin' down th' timber*** also means a hurried departure. When anyone isn't ***quite hard up th' back,*** he's cowardly. And if you can ***make a gent see daylight,*** you are making him understand. When you ***cool your heels,*** you're doing nothing.

High lopin' is easy going and gents who are ***small potatoes*** don't amount to much in their community. When you get so mad you can ***kick an anvil,*** you're plenty angry! To ***roll your hoop*** is to attend to your own affairs and let other peoples' alone. And when you say a gent hasn't ***sense enough to pound sand in a rat hole,*** that feller is downright ***igerunt.*** A 'puncher with ***a skin full*** is drunk. And a *wild goose chase* is a fruitless hunt. ***Ridin' high lines*** is cutting a swipe in society. A spot ***where you can hear uh ol' cow switch her tail*** is free of noise.

Anyone who doesn't ***give a whoop*** has no regards for consequences. If ***the plow stands,*** there's no work being done. When you hear a gent say ***I cleaned his plow,*** you will know that he has given someone a walloping. To leave without saying ***yes* or *no*** means you will leave without saying goodbye. When a gent leaves ***like heel flies were after him*** his speed is something to be marveled at. If you say ***you can put that down in your little red book,*** your listener may take it or leave it. ***Rollin' up a ball of yarn*** is completing a job. To ***win hands down*** means winning easily.

When you ***wouldn't trust anybody as far as you can throw a bull by its tail*** you haven't a great deal of confidence in the one referred to. If you ***bide the time*** you are waiting. And a feller who doesn't know ***split beans from coffee*** is very dumb. ***To get th' lay of the land*** is to look-over the country. Something ***fyancy*** is extremely nice. And ***some several things*** is more than one. ***Flexible brandin' irons*** may be used in making several different brands into one. When you ***wrop a gun barrel*** around a man's head, he's likely to have a severe headache. To ***get a feller's goat*** is to flabbergast him to where he's speechless.

When it's ***muddy enough to bog a snipe,*** you'll realize there's ***some several*** days of rain. ***No skin off'n his nose*** means it isn't any of that person's business. To ***shag all over hell's half acre*** is to cover some territory. When a man who has been sick recovers to the point where ***he's all healed up an' haired over,*** there's no further worry. If he's ***full of sass an' vinegar,*** you'll know he is well. Anyone who is as ***crochety as a chuckawalla*** is very easily offended. ***Not by a jug full*** is the limit on anything or effort. When you ***rowel a cayuse from ears to rump and from brisket to flank,*** you spur one side from the ears back and the other from the chest to flank.

If you hear a gent ***bellerin' like a boogered yealin' bull,*** you'll know that person is badly scared. If you ***haint got grit enough to kill a nit at a grayback rodeo,*** you're utterly spineless. If a gent is ***notched off,*** he's killed and somebody adds another notch to the butt of their six-gun. To ***kick over the traces*** is to rebel against anything. And if you see a feller ***jerk a saddle off'n a horse an' beat him on th' rump with th' bridle bits,*** that cayuse is gettin' a real ***larrupin'.*** When you say ***don't start cloudin' up,*** you mean don't get mad. ***Takin' th' country by an' large*** is taking the country on an average.

If you see a man ***comin' like a bat out of hell,*** he's doing some fancy traveling. When anything ***don't hold water,*** place no confidence in it. ***See can you*** is a Western expression meaning "if you can." ***Hold your hoss—tuck in your shirt tail*** is a command to be patient. When you ***open a bag o' talk*** you start a conversation. Beware of a gent who ***sharpens his tomahawk***—he's lookin' for trouble. To ***give up to ghost*** is to die. When you ***do your dangest,*** you're putting forth a supreme effort. A thin-faced gent wearing a wide-brimmed sombrero ***looks like a toad under a cabbage leaf.*** Two of ***the same stripe*** mean two alike.

Gander-shanks is a long-legged gent. When you keep ***a tight check rein*** on your temper, you'll stay out of trouble. To have ***a yeller streak from collar to crupper*** means you are a rank coward. ***A wood cuttin' bee*** is a timberland celebration. When you have ***an axe to grind*** you have something to settle with another person. To ***gather-up the loose ends*** is to understand all details of a proposition. When a gent ***gets rubbed-down with a stake pin,*** he gets larruped with a picket pin. To ***pull up stakes and leave*** means to take everything you own when you go. ***Starting from scratch*** is commencing at the beginning. ***A cowslip without a calf*** is a married woman who has no children.

Seeing ***th' riggin' of th' game*** is understanding all angles of a preposition. When a feller sounds ***like a bull cart squeakin'*** when he signs, his voice is terrible. To ***grab anyone by their hocks and bodaciously wrop 'em around a cottonwood, yonder,*** is considerable exertion. If you ***go down th' road talkin' to yourself*** you're worried or somethin'. When you ***set a heap of store*** of anything you regard it highly. To see a gent ***with his bootleg filled with ca'tridges*** is to see a man prepared for trouble. ***Stickin' like a chigger rash*** is showing considerable perseverance. When a cowboy ***swaps his saddle for a sheep hook*** he's disgraced among his brethren. And when a judge ***throws th' book*** at a prisoner, said felon receives the maximum sentence.

To ***notch your sights on a feller's brisket*** is to point to a gun at his chest. Weather ***colder'n a snake's heart*** is very cold.

When ***hell's to pay and no pitch hot,*** there's trouble galore. A gent ***battln' his eyes like a toad in a hail storm*** is winkin' 'em sort-of fast. The same goes for a ***toad eatin' fire.*** When you're ***safe as in god's own pocket,*** you have nothing to fear. Anything as ***stiff as a wet rope*** is quite stiff. If there's ***hell with the rough side out*** going on, trouble submerges you. ***Big swimmin'*** is a flooded river. To engage in a ***corpse and cartridge occasion*** is to take part in a shoot-out.

If you ***whistle and roll on by*** you don't stop to say howdy. A gent who has his boots ***polished with goose grease*** is somewhat slicked-up. To ***square through a crowd*** is to force one's way. Anyone as ***proud as a calf with two tails*** is some proud. And to ***savvy the badger*** is to understand. A team of horses which ***spanks along*** is a lively one. When a gent is ***as alert as a pinon jay,*** he'd be hard to surprise. A ***blaze-face sorrel*** is a reddish colored cayuse with a splash of white on it face. To ***settle his hash*** is to finish that person for keeps. As ***tense as a pointed quail*** is some tense.

A feller with a ***thorn-like smile*** should be avoided. To ***collapse like a busted tent pole*** is to fold in the middle. When a gent ***cuts his wolf loose,*** he's looking for trouble. And to know a country ***like the inside of grandma's pantry*** is to be well acquainted with that section. To ***high-tail it like a jackrabbit express,*** your departure is a distinct blur. ***Salt bush*** and ***goblin mesquite*** grow in the desert. When anything is ***as dry as a buzzard's shin bone*** there's no moisture whatever. Horses ***mumble in their nose bags*** when they're feeding. A gal what's ***as cute as a bag full of nuggets*** is easy on your eyes. The joke's on a gent when he says ***that's a hoss on me.***

A ***clay-yellow*** coloring or ***clay-bank*** is a term applied to horses of that color. ***Jacal*** is the Spanish term for a hut or shanty. A ***rosetted, rich brown rig*** is full-stamped horse gear. A cowboy is surprised or dismayed when he says ***hell's cinders! Headstalls*** is horse headgear. When you ***set in a game*** you take a hand or interfere in another's quarrel. And to tell a gent something ***to his teeth,*** you're not mincing words. Anything which fails ***to set well*** fails to please. When a feller ***gets his*** he receives his just dues. To ***shuffle cowhides,*** you drive or herd cattle. And when you're ***long on patience*** you aren't easily irritated.

A ***coffin filler*** is a gent apt with guns. A critter ***real prime*** has reached the peak of good condition. To ***hatch-up*** is to plan. ***High and mighty*** is a term applied to gents who regard themselves highly. To ***hold out*** is to withhold or fail to give out. When you ***pan out less'n nothing*** you're absolutely worthless. When the mud is deep enough to ***bog a saddle blanket,*** the mud reached above the horse's belly. If you're ***out in th' sand an' sinkin' fast,*** there's little to hope for. ***Upped an' done it*** is an impulsive action. To ***bust a seam*** or ***bust a tug*** is putting forth a supreme effort. When you ***get the dirty end of the stick*** you receive a raw deal. A gent who gets ***dusted, front and back,*** is shot through the body. ***Shot where th' galluses cross*** means just what that.

When a feller yells that ***he's from th' salt forks of bitter creek,*** he's double-tough. If you see a man ***travelin' so fast he has to turn sidew'ys to keep from flying,*** that hombre is doin' some tall moving. To ***tack a gent's hide on the barn door*** is to expose, overpower or whip him. ***Whole hog or none*** is to wager everything or nothing, to commit entirely or step away.

A ***sin-steeped-son-of-satan*** is a man beyond redemption. A ***sage hen*** what's as ***purty as a back bar picture*** is a gal who is easy to gaze upon. To ***think twice*** is to be cautious. ***Off'n th' deep end and no goin' back*** means you're in dire trouble with no chance of getting out. ***The way he did it was a caution*** refers to a clever performance. And ***sommers off th' other side o' hell*** is quite a distance away.

Anything ***blacker than th' ace of spades*** isn't white by any stretch of the imagination. And if a feller is ***busier than a bee in a tar bucket*** or is ***hoppin' like a toad in a wagon rut*** he's doing some stirring about. From the mining country comes an expression regarding a man's bravery: ***he assays less'n no guts at all.*** To have ***lived in a country since them hills were holes in th' ground*** is to have been there a long time. A gent who ***looks like somethin' rolled outa th' drag end of a stampede*** is considerable messed up. To ***let th' wolf loose*** is to open hostilities. And when one feller goes after another ***like a bitin' shoat after a bare shin,*** you may be assured he intends to do bodily harm. To ***be in a split stick*** is to be in dire trouble.

When you ***wet your guzzle*** you're drinking. To ***eat a man raw*** would be some undertaking. If someone ***looks like he'd been worked over by a flock of she wildcats in whelpin' time,*** his appearance isn't too good. To ***blow like quarter horse*** means you're out of breath from running. Anything ***as tough as a boiled owl*** would be difficult to chew. A gent who didn't have on ***enough clothes to pad a crutch or wat a shotgun shell*** was most nigh naked. To ***beat th' corral dust out of your Durham*** is to remove dust from your pockets. Anyone ***as solemn as a tree full of young owls*** is a comical sight. But if that same person ***looks as wise as a tree of young owls,*** his appearance is awe inspiring.

To ***get a winder in you skull*** is to be shot through the head. A gent what's ***some reckless*** has no regard of consequences. ***Vamoose*** for ***the cedar brakes*** and ***unravel some ca'tridges*** is to go into the cedar timber and do some shooting. When a rancher's ***calves don't suck th' right cows,*** he must be a rustler. A ***slick-lookin' filly*** is a beautiful gal or a trim young mare. To ***be planted out on boot hill*** is to be buried with the hombres who died with their boots on. When a ***herd is rode down for beddin'*** they are halted for the night's rest. Cattle milling in the middle of a river is called a ***merry-go-round.***

To ***be heeled*** is to ***pack a cutter.*** In other words you are armed with a six-shooter. A gent with ***an itchy trigger finger*** should be avoided. When you

throw down on anybody, you cover them with a gun. If an hombre says he's ***plumb sway-backed and bow-legged from packin' his kak,*** you'll know he's carried his saddle a long distance and is tired. To ***pack enough hardware to cause kidney sores*** is to go heavily armed. When you go after a feller ***red-eyed an' a-grinnin'*** you are in earnest. A ***gun tipper*** is a gent who fires through the open bottom of his gun holster.

To ***blow a gent's light out*** is to kill him. A ***mammy*** is a cow with a calf. Also referred to as ***wet stuff. Wooshers*** and ***woolies*** are hogs and sheep. It is unhealthy to ***lean against a passin' bullet. Hell bent for election*** is traveling fast. And a ranch operated by a woman is termed a ***squaw outfit.*** A ***furrin' gent*** is a newcomer from another locality. ***Hipped around*** is to turn the body without moving the feet. ***Hep to*** anything is to understand. A ***tinker's damn*** doesn't amount to a great deal. ***Steel-dust*** is the coloring of a horse. Roan, sorrel, buttermilk, palomino, gray, bay, flea-bit, dun, chestnut, dapple-gray are also colors of cayuses.

GLOSSARY of COW-COUNTRY VOCABULARY

-A-

aced: Killed with one shot; overcome by a single attempt.

ace high: The best of everything; tops; supreme.

ache: To complain; grumble; grouse; find fault.

acion: Stirrup leathers on saddle. Spanish.

acorn calf: A scrubby calf; a weakling; a runt.

actin' like a yearlin' gone loco: Without sense; reckless; foolish; careless; without reason.

adios: Goodbye. Spanish word adopted in Southwest.

admire: Wish for; want; desire. "I'd admire tuh do that."

adobe: 'dobe: A brown clay used for making sun-dried bricks. Straw is mixed with the wet mass to hold bricks together more firmly when dry. Due to affinity of the Mexican border country, adobe houses a hundred years old are common. When exposed to a steady rain the adobe brick will return to its original status unless protected by plaster.

aig: Egg.

aim: Intent to do something. "I aim tuh go over Carizosa way."

airin' his guts: Airin' his paunch; talking volubly; telling all he knows.

airtights: Canned food of any kind.

alfal uise: Alfalfa. Excellent food for fatting stock.

alforja: Saddlebags; canvas or leather bags lashed to pack saddle. Also, *alforki* Spanish term. See *paniers.*

alkali lick: Similar to a *salt lick,* which see.

alkalied: Acclimated to the desert.

allus: Always.

amble along: To move slowly; take one's time. See *june along.*

amigo: Friend. adios, amigo: Goodbye, friend. Spanish.

ancient: An old man; oldster; oldtimer; wart hog; scissorbill.

angora chaps: Wool covered chaps used in northwest. When working in desert country the cowboy usually wears *batwing chaps,* which see.

animal: An "animal" is usually a horse while a "critter" is a cow.

anthrax: A virulent disease caused from lack of water, usually fatal to livestock.

anti-godlin: Crooked; cross- or sidewise; slaunchwise.

aparejo: Pack saddle. Spanish term adopted in Southwest.

Arbuckle: A brand of coffee popular in cow country. It sold for two-bits per package and in return for the fac-simile signature the manufacturers (the cowboys called it a "made" coffee) gave away premiums. Those of the oldtimers who could read knew every word on the printed label, frontwards and backwards.

arbuckle: A tenderfoot; newcomer; greenhorn; see *pilgrim*

Arkansas toothpick: A long, pointed knife; a Bowie knife.

arrowweed: A straight, reed-like plant growing in damp canyons and on open desert to a height of eight or ten feet.

arroyo: A dry stream bed; see *gully: wash: draw: coulee: canyon.*

artillery: Firearms; hardware; See *gun.*

ary: Any.

A.T.: Arizona territory: History written in blood to the tune of blasting guns, cloaked Arizona in her mantle of romance. The story writer of today has an ideal locale in this hunting ground of fierce Apaches and cold-eyed outlaws.

A-tall: At all.

auger: The owner or boss of an outfit; see *ramrod;* also, *boss.*

auger the cook: A favorite pastime of cowboys. Means to talk to or visit with the cook, hoping to finagle a handout or get to play on the coffee pot.

-B-

bach: Bachelor; A Sourdough; an unmarried gent who does his own cooking; to live minus matrimonial fetters.

back-fire: To set an opposing fire. Prairie or range fires destroy the grass. To combat the spreading flame, fires are set ahead and forced to burn back toward the advancing blaze; also, a kick-back.

back jockeys: The wide, flat leathers behind saddle cantle; bastos.

back trail: To retrace one's steps; to go back.

bad actor: A bad man; a horse hard to manage.

bad eye: The mean, treacherous eye of man or animal.

badlands: Rough, desolate, broken country; the honkatonk district of a good-sized cow town.

bad man: An odious person; bad hombre; tough gent; a salty feller.

baile: A dance; ball; See *shindig.* Spanish term popular with cow country folk.

bait: Food; chuck; grub; vittles; chow; duff; scoff. See *spoon vittles;* also, *son-of-a-gun-in-a-sack.*

bait uh vittles: Bait o' grub; a full meal even though it be only frijoles.

band: A group or herd of horses. Never refers to cattle.

bandy-legged: Bow legged; warped legs; legs that fit a horse: pipe-stem legs; spindly shanks. See *bow-legs.*

bangtails: Range horses; mustangs; wild, unbroken horses; fuzztails; fantails; broncs, broomies.

barboquejos: Chin straps on cowboy's sombrero, usually rawhide.

bar dog: The bartender in a saloon or cantina.

barefoot coffee: Black coffee to which neither cream nor sugar had been added.

barefoot horse: One without shoes.

bar fly: A loafer in a saloon; hanger-on; a moocher of drinks.

barrel cactus: A large, barrel-shaped cactus with heavy ribs and spines, five to six feet high.

basin: An oval or circular valley or depression usually containing water.

bastos: The area behind saddle cantle. Spanish. See *back jockeys.*

battin' an eye: "He shot the killer without battin' an eye."

bat out o' hell: Expresses fast traveling. "He left for the tall uncut like a bat out o' hell."

batty: Crazy; locoed; "teched in th' haid;" "He's plumb batty."

batwing chaps: Wide leather coverings worn over trousers for protection while riding through brush or cactus. To complete the ensemble the cowboy might wear a leather jacket, sombrero, leather gloves, leather wristlets and tapadero stirrups, thus fully "leathering" him against cat-claw, etc.; "Chaps" is contracted from chaparejos; chaps; chivarras; see *chaps* and *angora chaps.*

batwing doors: The swinging, half-doors of a saloon.

bayed: Cornered; treed; dammed or backed-up as water.

bayo coyote: A dun or buckskin horse. See *line-back.*

bed down: Riding-down a moving herd or cattle and bunching them for the night's rest and grazing. When the cattle are bedded-down, the night herders go on duty.

bed-ground: The spot selected for halting a moving herd for the night. See *bed down.*

bedroll: The cowboy's bed. Usually packed behind saddle except on round-up when it is carried in bed wagon or by pack animal. See *soogan;* also, *bed wagon.*

bed wagon: Wagon used to haul bedding of cowboys on round-up. Also, hoodlum wagon. A pack mule is sometimes referred to as a "wagon" when used for this purpose.

beef: A steer suitable for marketing; to complain; to growl; to belly-ache; see *ache.*

beef book: Tally book; record book or herd on ranch. See *tally.*

beef cut: The steers which are "cut out" or separated from the main herd and ready for marketing.

began owl hootin: Took to outlawry. See *hoot owler* and *owlhooter.*

bell mare: A mare which runs with cavvy or remuda with a bell attached to her neck to facilitate location of horse herd. See *remudera.*

belly wash: Near-beer; soda pop; also, baloney; hot air; guff.

bench brand: A figure, symbol or character resting on top of an inverted bench or bracket. See *character brand.*

bend: To turn or swing a herd of cattle while on the move. It is the duty of *point riders* to "bend" or guide the herd.

big bend country: a portion of West Texas in the big bend of the Rio Grande river devoted to cattle raising. This is the scene of countless stirring events which helped to make cow history.

biscuit shooter or **roller:** Waitress in a cheap restaurant; hash-slinger; also, the camp cook.

bit: See *bridle bit* and *spade bit.* The snaffle bit is a jointed bit. The Arizona grazing bit is a small bit with a curb in the mouthpiece. The boy from Wyoming aptly calls the spade bit a "stomach-pump," as it might so act in the hands of a rough or careless rider. A "bit" is also 12½¢ in money; two-bits is a quarter.

bit the dust: Landed in the dust by either being shot down or thrown from a bucking horse; grabbed or clawed dirt; see *chewed dirt.*

blab: A square board attached to a calf's mouth to prevent sucking; also, to run at the mouth or talk too freely.

black chaparral: A stiff-limbed, thorny shrub or bramble growing in thickets in Southwest.

black jack: A card game, sometimes called 21; a stunted, stiff-limbed species of oak growing in Southwest, excellent for firewood.

blanca: White. Spanish.

blanket buck: A male blanket Indian.

blanket Indian: An Indian who persists in wrapping himself in the folds of a gaudy blanket. The degree of prosperity is to be judged by the fineness of blanket, worn alike by *bucks* and *squaws.* Even in warm summer weather the women folk us very heavy shawls.

blaze face: A horse with a splash of white on its face.

blind-bucker: a horse that bucks or plunges blindly into a corral fence or other obstruction.

blinders: Blinkers; leather screens on bridle, used on horses easily startled by objects along the trail.

blinding: Covering a bronc's eyes to facilitate saddling; sacking; see *sacked 'em out.*

blind trail: A false trail; a dim or indistinct trail.

blind trap: Corral built to trap wild horses. These corrals are usually quite large with fan-shaped wings. The wild range horses or mustangs are hazed into the wings then driven into the corral.

blizzard: A storm with high, freezing winds, snow and sleet; a tornadic blast; see *blue whistler* and *cold as a wedge.*

blocker loop: An extremely large loop in a lariat. Originated by John Blocker of Texas.

blot: To change or "work over" a brand from one design to another. For this purpose the rustler sometimes used a knife, or acid, or a hot iron and a wet blanket. See *brand blotcher.*

blow: To pant or puff; to rest when winded; "They stopped the horses and let them "blow."; also, to brag or boast.

blowed in: arrived: blew in: also, spent all of money.

blow-up: To commence bucking; see *boil over, uncork* and *onwind.*

blue whistler: Freezing, whistling weather; see *blizzard.*

bodaciously: All; entirely; total; also, naturally. "I'll bodaciously pick you up an' wrop you around one o' them cottonwoods, yonder."

body spin: A trick roping term; the reata is spun over the head and brought down over body of roper.

bog camp: Camp near a bog hole where cattle are apt to become mired down. See *tail-up.*

bog down: To mire down in mud. Also, to be at a loss for speech. "I jest nachurally bog down when I talk to gals."

bogged his head: Hung his head; said of a bucking horse when he drops his head between forelegs and *uncorks.* A "winding-up" process.

bog rider: The cowboy who rides to various bog holes and *tails-up* or drags out cattle which are mired in the mud.

boiled shirt: Stiff, starched shirt; b'iled shirt; baldface. Unpopular among cowboys. See *fried shirt.*

boil over: To commence bucking. See *uncork, onwind, bogged his head.*

bold as a jackass: Brazen; without modesty; an un-shrinking violet; nervy.

bone orchard: Western term for graveyard. See *boot hill.*

bonnet strings: Buckskin thongs used to hold sombrero on head. See *barboquejos.*

boogery: Skittish; spooky; nervous; flighty; easily frightened.

book count: The selling of a herd of cattle from ranch records without actual count. On final tally, the buyer ofttimes comes up short.

boot hill: A frontier cemetery. So named because those buried there usually "cashed-in" with their boots on. All old-time western towns have a boot hill graveyard. One near Tombstone, Arizona, has quite a population. See *bone orchard.*

bored: Shot; salivated; ventilated; plugged; dusted; see LEAD PIZEN.

borrow: A satirical term meaning to steal.

bosque: Brush or trees. Spanish. Cattle running in brushy country are called boskeys.

boss: The ranch owner or representative of owner; the foreman; head man; head taster; auger; big auger; big noise; big he; he-coon; king-pin; rod; ramrod.

botched brand: A bad job of brand changing or *blotting;* sometimes very humiliating to the rustler. See *blot.*

bottle plant: The desert trumpet. Grows to a height of 3 feet.

boughten: Cowboy version of bought.

bow-legged: The indelible trademark of the cow country. Anyone who spends years in the saddle develops bowed or warped legs. The length of a cowboy's service is usually shown by how well his legs fit a horse. Bowed legs are as common in the cow country as is a man with two eyes. Incidentally, the man folks are not alone in this parenthesis-leg line-up.

brace: To confront; challenge.

Brahma bull: Brama or Bramma bull; a humped beast of foreign origin used largely for rodeo work. Very difficult to ride. When the Brahma succeeds in throwing a rider, he usually attacks him sometimes with serious results. Ridden with *surcingle* because a saddle will not stay put.

brand: The mark of ownership. The brand is burned on the animal's side, hip or shoulder by means of a *branding iron* or *running iron,* well heated. There are thousands of different brands, some of them very famous, made up of letter or figure combinations or characters or symbols. N Bar N; Circle Dot; Lazy S; Rocking Y; T Bench; Rafter O; Swinging C; etc. See *ear mark.*

brand: Hair brand. A phoney brand made by cattle rustlers by plucking or cutting hair from critter's hide into the desired pattern. Acid is used to burn brand into the hide. The brand made with a hot iron shows through on the inside of hide, the others do not.

brand: A man's character; disposition; temperament; intentions.

brand blotcher or **burner:** The slick-fingered gent who "works over" other brands into his own. See *blot - botched brand.*

branding iron: The instrument used in branding or marking stock with sign of ownership; a "set" or stamp iron.

brass hat: An important person.

bratty: With characteristics of a "brat."

break 'im of suckin' eggs: Teach him a lesson; educate him.

break in two: To commence bucking. See *boil over: uncork: onwind: bogged his head: ruck-off.*

breaking pen: The corral where horses are broke to ride.

breaking tank: Same as above.

breast strap: A strap fitting across horse's breast in use on saddles in mountainous country. Also, part of pack saddle rigging.

breeching: Part of saddle rigging that fits around horse's breech for use in hilly country. The breast strap goes fore, the breeching goes aft.

brew: Plot or plan anything.

bridle bit: The metal bar on bridle fitting into horse's mouth which aids rider in controlling mount. See *bit: Spanish bit: spade bit.*

bridle wise: A horse which responds to bridle control; knowing exactly what is wanted.

bring tuh heel: Bring under control.

broke in two: See *break in two.*

broke the mold: Destroyed the pattern.

bronc: From Spanish *bronco,* meaning rough or wild; a wild or semi-broken horse, sometimes a steer. Also called bronk, broncho, bronco, braunk.

bronc buster: A cowboy who takes the rough edges off a bronc by teaching him the use of saddle, bridle, riding, etc.; also called bronc peeler, snapper, stomper. See *man.*

broncho steer: A wild one.

broom tail: A scrubby range horse; same as *bang tail:* Broomie.

brush popper: A cowboy accustomed to driving cattle in brushy country; a brush-snapper; brush-hand.

brush splitters: Cattle of the brush country.

buck: A male Indian, young or old. See *blanket buck.*

buck: To pitch; ruck; jump; sunfish; fence-row; stiff-leg. The action of a horse or steer in trying to throw rider.

buckaroo: Buckeroo; A term applied to cowboys, especially in Nevada, California and Oregon.

buckboard: A light, four-wheeled vehicle used in the west.

bucking roll: The padded front of a saddle designed expressly for riding bucking horses. See *slicker roll.*

bucking wood: Sawing wood with a bucksaw.

buck jump: A tenderfoot term referring to the action of a bucking horse. "A horse what buck jumps."

buck knees: Knock knees. Opposite of *bow-legged.*

buck teeth: Protruding front teeth. Billy the Kid had 'em.

bueno: Good. Spanish.

buenas dias: Good day. **buenas noches:** Good night.

buffalo: To bluff; over-awe; perplex; intimidate; also, the animal itself.

buffalo chips: Dried buffalo dung, used by oldtimers for fuel. See *cow chips* and *prairie coal.*

buffalo gun: A rifle of heavy calibre used in hunting buffalo.

buffalo soldiers: A term given by Indians to Negro soldiers.

bug juice: Whiskey; likker; panther sweat; pizen; snake remedy; dynamite; tarantula juice; firewater, etc.

buggy boss: A tenderfoot ranch owner who rides in a buggy instead of on horseback.

build a loop: To form a lariat loop see *shake out a loop.*

build a quirly: To roll a cigarette from the *makin's;* also spelled querly.

bull: Spoof; blarney. The male of the species cattle.

bull cook: A construction camp flunky, chamber-maid or police-up man. He has nothing to do with the cooking of meals except in small outfits. See *swamper.*

bull dogging: A sport among cowboys. A rider races his horse beside running steer, leaps to critter's head and seizes horns. By twisting them to the side, the steer falls - perhaps.

bull into: To act without thinking; to be impulsive or rash.

bull nurse: The cowboy who accompanies a shipment of cattle to destination.

bull whacker: A driver of oxen, while a *mule skinner* is a driver of mules or horses.

bum steer: False directions; misinformation; wrong pew.

bunch: To drive cattle or horses into a herd; cattle are referred to as a "bunch" while horses are a "band."

bunch quitter: A critter that persists in leaving its fellows by sneaking away through brush or undergrowth.

bunch grassers: People living in the western foothills.

bunk: Sleeping quarters. They never have beds on a ranch - they are always bunks.

bunkhouse: Cowboy's housing quarters on the ranch in which are arranged the bunks. There is usually a long table with lamps at either end, a few chairs, etc.

burned his feet off: Hurried; lost no time; sped.

burn 'em down: Shoot them down!

burn powder: To shoot.

burn th' breeze: To ride fast; to hurry.

burnt out: Tired or sick of.

burro: A donkey; booraw; desert canary. He won this last name on account of his voice. Also, a wooden frame used to support a saddle when not in use.

The burro is without doubt the most reliable, most unreliable faithful quadruped ever cussed and chased by a westerner. The settlement of the arid country centers around the burro as he was and is the boon companion of prospectors and oldtimers. The discovery of many rich gold and silver mines can be traced directly to this little animal. One old miner, testifying in a Tonopah, Nevada, damage suit, stated that he had prospected five years and hunted his pack burros twenty-five, thus qualifying his as an expert witness - in burrology.

burro-weed: A desert plant.

bushwaw!: An exclamation of scorn or disbelief.

bushwhacker: An ambusher.

bust: To break horses to ride; a wild fling; a whing-ding.

busted flat: Without funds. Not uncommon with cowboys.

buster: A bronc twister; a breaker of wild horses. See *man.*

butte: A lone hill or prominence. Butte, Montana, is built on one.

butter out of an oil can: Has reference to a man who might be dirty or neglectful of his personal appearance but who is all white (clean) inside.

button: A boy; yonker; kid; young feller; young'un; young squirt; frying size; see *squirt.*

button your lip: Shut up!; dry up; stop yapping; shut yore yap; close yore trap.

buzzard: An odious person; a scavenger of the hawk family which lives off carrion. Wheeling circles of buzzards is a sure sign that some creature is dead or in distress. The lower the circle, the weaker the unfortunate.

buzzard bait: Dead. "Guess the old boy is buzzard bait by now."

by a long shot: Supreme attempt; the ultimate effort.

- C -

cable: Rope used in make up of temporary rope corral for holding remuda on open range.

cache: A hideout; to conceal or hide anything.

cactus boomers: Wild brush cattle: wild steers; facetiously called "salty oxen;" see *wild ladings.*

cactus-haired: Bristly haired; a tough gent; salty.

calf crop: Yearly increase in herd of cattle. While the farmer estimates his yearly gain in the size of his grain crop, the cowman figures his gain in the calf crop.

calf rope: Give up or acknowledge defeat. "He yelled, 'Calf rope.'"

calf 'round: To loaf; be idle; to moon around, as a cowboy in love is supposed to do.

calf slobbers: Whipped cream; meringue; cake frosting; the what'zit that is slobbered on top of a lemon or cream pie.

calico: A pony splashed with different colors, usually black and white or brown and white; a pinto; paint-hoss. It also refers to a girl. See *gal* and *sage hen.*

caliente: Hot. **agua caliente:** hot water. Spanish.

California rigging: The single cinch or center-fire saddle. California, Oregon and Nevada mostly retain the Spanish methods of handling cattle, while Texas, Wyoming Montana, etc. have names and methods peculiar to their territory, thus:

California-Nevada Texas-Montana-Wyoming

The center-fire sadde - Double rigged saddle

Cattle worked in corral - Cattle worked on range

Buckaroo becomes a - Cowboy

Dally men us a 60 ft. - Tie men us a 35 ft. whale- line rope,

rawhide reata lariat or maguey

Parada becomes main herd

Orejana becomes slick ear
caviada becomes remuda
Batwing chaps become angora chaps
pizen is drank simply as likker.

California sox: Barefoot; without shoes or stockings.

called his hand: Accepted his challenge or dare.

callin': Courting; girlin'; sparkin' gallin'.

calor: Heat; warm weather. Spanish.

camino: A road. **El camino real**: The king's highway. Spanish.

camp on a trail: To follow doggedly, persistently.

camping on their hocks: Following them closely.

campo santo: A cemetery. Spanish.

Canadian river: A western river. Spanish Conquistadores and all the adventurous swashbucklers who followed them, camped and fought on the banks of this famous stream.

candle-wood: The ocotillo. A desert bush growing six feet high.

canned cow: Canned milk; embalmed cow. See *air-tights.*

canon or canyon: A narrow gorge with steep sides.

can't hold a candle t' him: Can't compare with him.

cantle: The rear raised part of a saddle.

canvas hotel: A tent; a stretched tarpaulin; see *tarp.*

carcel: A jail; prison; see *juzgado.*

caress with a whiffletree: To strike.

cash-in: To die; to make a clean-up; to reimburse.

cat-claw: A bush, often mistaken for small mesquite, covered with small, sharp spines. Grows to ten feet.

catgut: A rope; see *reata* and *lariat.*

cavvy: The horse herd; see *remuda;* the extra cowboy mounts herded together; caviada; cavvieard; cavvyada; cavvyard.

cavvy-wrango: The horse herder of a cavvy; see *wrangle* and *horse wrangler.*

cayuse: A pony or mustang; sometimes applied to horses in general.

cedar: A six-shooter. So named when having cedar plates on grip. See *gun.*

cedar breakers: Cattle frequenting the cedar breaks high on the mountainsides.

center-fire: Saddle having but one cinch or girth; single-barreled and single-rigged. Also, called California rigging.

chaps: Chaparejos; chivarras; skeleton overalls; leather or haired covering worn over trousers to protect legs from brush and cold while riding. See *angora chaps; batwing chaps.*

character brands: Brands formed from symbols or characters. See *brand.*

chew dirt: To get thrown from a bucking horse. "Chaw grit."

chicken-livered: Cowardly; without nerve; yeller; no guts.

chico: Little; small boy.

chili: Pepper. Spanish. An extremely hot Mexican food; also, a derisive name for a Mexican.

chili eater: A Mexican.

chinkin' in: Filling in during an emergency; aiding; helping.

Chinook: A wind coming from the west is supposed to have some connection with the warm Japan current. It takes the life out of cattle causing them to become exhausted. The blow usually lasts three days and when followed by freezing weather, the results to stock is disastrous. Unless the cattle are "tailed up" they freeze to death. Also termed "snow-hog" and "banana-ripener."

chin th' ground: Same as *chew dirt.*

chiquita: Little one.

chivaree: Charivari; celebration after a cowboy's wedding.

chive: A knife.

chola: A Mexican.

cholla: A cactus growing up to six feet high.

choosy: Particular. "That gal's all fired choosy."

chouse: To stir up unnecessarily; agitate; prod; chase. The rider who chouses cattle shows incompetence.

choke the horn: To grab and hold on to the saddle horn when riding a bucking horse.

chuck: Food; grub; duff; groceries; scoff; vittles; see *bait.*

chuck-a-luck: A gambling game played with dice.

chuckawalla: Species of lizard inhabiting arid regions. Grows to a length of two feet, and two inches across back.

chuck box: Kitchen cabinet attached to rear of chuck wagon.

chuckline rider: A drifting cowboy following cow camps, thereby gaining free food and lodging. Sometimes honestly looking for work but often a bum or moocher; see *grubline rider* and *saddle tramp.*

chuck wagon: The wagon used to haul supplies during round-up. The cook's eminent domain. The chuck wagon is the center of activities on a trail drive or round-up.

cigarro: A cigarette. Spanish.

Cimarron: An historical Southwestern river; an outcast.

Cimmy: Contraction of above.

cinch: Cincha; the saddle girt or girth. A webbed or hair strap for holding saddle in place; something sure, certain or positive.

cinch bet: A sure thing; no chance to lose.

circle: To drive in a circle; *on circle:* On the circular drives which bring cattle into the round-up herd.

ciudad: City. Spanish.

claim: A government allotment of land; a homestead.

claim jumper: One who jumps or takes possession of another's claim; usually ends in a gunfight.

claw leather: Pull leather; grab leather; see *leather* and *choke the horn.* Seizing the saddle horn when riding a bucking horse. In rodeo work, one hand holds the reins and the other must be held in plain sight. "Clawing leather" disqualifies rider.

claybank: A clay-colored horse; drab or gray.

clean out a snake's nest: to raid an outlaw hangout.

clean-up: To wipe clean; profits; net gain; also, a mining term.

close-herd him: Watch him carefully; follow him closely.

cocklebur: A thorny weed growing in Southwest which, contacting a horse's tail, mats it into a solid mass. Burs may be removed by application of kerosine and profanity.

cocktail guard: The final night guard of the cattle herd and the one most heartily despised by cowboys.

coffee what'll float a wedge: Strong, black coffee; coffee heavy enough to float an egg; see *Arbuckle: barefoot coffee; creekful of coffee* and *egg float.*

cold as a wedge: Plenty cold weather.

cold blood: A native range horse with mustang strain. See *hot blood.*

cold-deck: To cheat or trap.

cold-footed: Cowardly; without nerve; spineless.

cold-jawed: A horse unused or unresponsive to bridle signals.

cold turkey: The facts; plain, unvarnished truth.

colorado: Red. Spanish.

Colt: A popular make of firearms. The history of the west centers around the *Colt.* See *gun.*

colt: A young horse.

comb: To spur a horse to make him buck; to "curry him out"; see *rake* and *rowel.*

come again: What?; repeat that.

come apart: The action of a bucking horse.

come and get it or I'll throw it out: "Chuck"; The cook's call to meals.

come a-smokin': To come out a-shootin'; a warning to have guns ready at a certain time.

c'm'on: Come on; comeuppances; airs; false pretenses; putting on.

conchas: Shells. Spanish. Applied to metal ornaments on chaps, holsters, hat bands, belts and saddle skirts.

confab: A talk; discussion. See *pow-wow; talky-talk; palaver; wau-wau.*

conk: To strike on the head. See *tunk.*

conk out: To die. See *cash-in.*

cookie: Cook; the ranch or camp cook. Also referred to as grub wrangler, belly cheater, dough roller, old lady, Susie.

coon-up: To climb. "He cooned-up the tree."

corazone: Sweetheart. A word popular with romantic cowboys. Spanish.

cornfed granger: A dirt farmer; see *fool hoe man; churn twister* and *sod buster.* The farmer who came on to the range land, fenced it off and utilized the choicest water holes, was at one time not a popular citizen from the cowman's standpoint.

corporal: The boss of an outfit. Word not in common use.

corral: A pen to hold stock; to corral anything is to "catch" it. The corral is usually built of heavy timbers or logs so as to withstand the onslaught of a vicious horse or wild bull. The *rope corral* is a temporary corral made with a cable and used for holding the remuda on open range. See *breaking pen.*

corregidor: Mayor. Spanish.

corrida: To race. Spanish. Any outfit of cowboys.

cotton: To be friendly. Usually used negatively, as, "I never cottoned to him."

cottonwood fruit: A man hanged from the limb of a cottonwood tree. See *necktie party.*

couched in proper language: Anything told with emphasis; embellished with profanity.

couldn't see his pony's head: Because the pony was bucking so hard that his head was between forelegs. Also refers to a dark night or a gent packing a jag.

coulee: A stream bed, usually, dry, having inclined walls which are not so steep as those of a canyon.

cowboy: A herder of cattle; also called cow-hand; cow waddy; cowpuncher; cowpoke; cow chaser, etc. See *man.*

cowboy's dream: Anything fancy; elaborate.

cow camp: Temporary or permanent camp away from home ranch. See *line camp.*

cow chips: Dry cow dung. Makes a hot fire. See *buffalo chips* and *prairie coal.*

cow-chouser: A careless or inexperienced cowboy. See *chouse* and *man.*

cowhand caper: A cowboy dance. See *shindig.*

cow horse: A horse trained to work among cattle; cow pony. See *cutter.* The cow horse is usually a top horse.

cow: to make a cow is to make up a purse.

cowman: He who makes a business of raising cattle.

cow nurse: A derisive name for a cowboy, often causes a fight.

cow pony: See *cow horse* and *cutter.*

cowpuncher: A cowboy. Cattle are prodded or "punched" up the loading chute with a long, metal-tipped pole, hence the name "Cowpuncher." See *prod pole* and *man.*

coyote: A cowardly prairie wolf which preys upon calves, colts and injured or weakened animals; the term is also applied to an odious person. "He's a low-down, sneakin' coyote."

coyoted: Quit cold; deserted; backed down. See *rabbited.*

cracked down on him: Shot him; struck him.

crawl your hump: A declaration showing a willingness to fight or attack; also, a warning to beware; same as "hopping his hump." Supposedly originated by some old cactus-haired buffalo hunter. "I'll crawl yer hump if y' 'ain't keerful."

creased: The shooting of anyone wherein the bullet grazes the scalp.

creekful of coffee: Plenty coffee. The cowboy is a lover of coffee. If the cook is congenial, a huge pot of coffee is always ready for drinking. Whenever a man on night guard of the herd feels sleepy, he resorts to the coffee pot to restore wakefulness. This blackened coffee pot is an institution in cow-camps. See *Arbuckle: barefoot coffee: coffee what'll float a wedge: egg-float.*

crimp: Obstruct; stop; hinder. "I'll crimp that hombre, believe me."

critter: Contraction of "creature." Cowboys class all quadrupeds as critters.

crossed the ridge: Died. See *cashed in.*

crow bait: A scubby horse. See *wind-bellied maverick.*

crowding pen: The branding pen; small corral. See *corral.*

crow hop: The short, stiff-legged jumps of a horse; mild bucking.

crummy: Disreputable; run-down; shabby; shoddy; seedy.

crupper: Part of a harness; rigging or pack saddle to prevent pack from slipping forward. See *breast strap.*

cull: A discarded animal; to cull is to cut out or separate.

curly wolf: A tough gent; a bad hombre; see *salty.*

cuss words: (Mild) consarn; dag-nab; dad-burn; gosh awful; daggone. Perhaps it's the heat, the dust, the cold, or his grueling hours with stubborn, refractory animals; at any rate, the cowboy has developed a scorching vocabulary which is a marvel of invention. See *swear words.*

cut a shine: Acted up; showed off; strutted. "Old Walapai Pete shore cut a shine at the shindig."

cut back: To retrace; an inferior critter; a cull.

cut bank: A bank cut away by swift water. See *cut-wash.*

cut his cinches: Changed his mind; broke away; "burned all bridges behind him."

cut his sign: Crossed his trail; discovered traces of him.

cut out: To separate a particular critter from among many.

cutter: A cutting pony; a chopping horse. A trained cow pony or cow horse used in separating stock from the rounded-up herd. The cutter is of necessity an extremely clever and nimble horse. The instant he understands the urgings of his rider, he plunges after the steer which is to be driven from the herd and never gives up until that particular critter is separated from the others. The cow pony forces his way through the milling, bawling herd and drives the steer ahead of him, encouraging speed by vicious nips at the driven critter's hide. See *ketch dog.*

cutting grounds: The area selected in which to separate the stock of various owners from among the rounded-up herd.

cutting quirt: A thin leashed, biting hand whip. See *quirt.*

cut-wash: A cut bank; arroyo; coulee; draw; gully; swale; wash. The banks are cut away by the action of flooding water.

-D-

dab: To throw a rope; to loop or lasso.

dab his twine: Same as above.

daggone: A common cowboy term expressing amazement. "Well, daggone, I wouldn't a thunk it o' Pete."

daisy hand: A derisive term applied to cowboys which when so applied usually means a fight.

dally: dallie: dalla delta: In some parts of the west, California, Nevada, etc., the reata is not tied to the saddle horn but after a critter is roped, loop's of the reata are thrown or "dallied" around the horn to aid in holding. The cowboys using this method or roping are known as "dally men." The dally also refers to the saddle horn. "The dally man took several dallies around the horn."

damfino: Cowboy expression meaning, "I do not know."

dance on air: To be hanged; to stretch hemp at a neck-tie party; see *cottonwood fruit; necktie party.*

dashboards: The feet; also, the front of a buckboard or buggy.

day herder: Cowboy on duty watching cattle herd during daytime; the opposite of night herder on the graveyard and cocktail shifts. This job is not relished by the average cowboy.

deal from the bottom: To cheat at anything; underhand methods. See *cold-deck* and *skullduggery.*

dead shot: A sure thing; no chance of loss; dead sure.

deep in the wood: Sitting well down in the saddle: the pitching horse unable to buck him off; in the trough.

dehorn: To remove the horns of a cowbrute.

Derringer: A deadly pocket gun; a hideout gun. This type was popular years ago in the frontier towns and settlements.

desert canary: The burro; booraw. See *burro.*

desert holly: a desert shrub which grows to two feet high.

desert Lily: A true lily of the desert.

diamond hitch: A knot or loop in a rope very useful to the cowboy.

dicker: To bargain.

difficulty: A fight; argument; fracas; fracus; ruckus; dog-fight; trouble of any variety.

dinero: Money; frog-skins; cart wheels. Spanish.

'dobe: See adobe. "We 'dobe-walled him," means, "We shot him."

dofunny: An inconsequential article; a doodad; thingamajig.

dog fight: A free-for-all fight. See *difficulty.*

dogie: An orphaned or deserted calf. See *leppy.*

dog town: The burrows of prairie dogs. The "town" sometimes covers an area of several square miles. Dangerous to ride through as the horse may step into one of the holes and break a leg.

do it up brown: Do a job well; leave nothing unfinished.

don coyote: Don Quixote, the cowboy from La Mancha who tilted at windmills.

do'no: Do not know. See *damfino.*

don't give a copper-colored damn: Absolutely without interest.

double holstered gun belt: A gun belt carrying twin holsters, affected by "two-gun" men.

double catfits: Somewhat of an emotional ruckus.

dough belly: Whey-belly; a distended middle; see *pot-belly.*

doughgod: Dough god; biscuits fried in grease in a skillet. Should you eat three of these, then fall in a crack, you would drown.

dough roller: The cook; grub wrangler; biscuit shooter; see *cookie.*

drag: The rear of a moving herd. The riders who follow the herd are called drag or tail riders. A dirty, dusty, choking job, usually assigned to new or inexperienced riders. See *point rider: swing rider.*

drag it: Leave in a hurry; vamoose. See *light a shuck* and *light out.*

drag rider: The tail rider of a moving herd. See *drag: point rider: swing rider.*

draw: A gully: swale: arroyo. Also to unlimber your artillery.

drift: To wander aimlessly; in a storm, cattle turn and drift before the wind.

drift fence: A fence across a range to halt wandering cattle.

drive: To start a herd in motion; the herd as a whole.

dry camp: A camp without water. A frequent occurrence in the arid Southwest.

dry stuff: Steers; dry cows: see *mammy* and *wet stuff.*

dude: A tenderfoot; greener; greenhorn; a flashily dressed newcomer. See *pilgrim.*

dude ranch: A cow ranch given over to city people.

dude wrangler: A cowboy working on a Dude Ranch who rides herd on the dudes - male and female. A thankless and nerve-wracking job as any good cowpoke will testify. There are certain compensations, however, which go to make the life bearable. Cowboys get lonesome, too.

duff: Food; chuck; grub; chow; scoff; see *bait.*

duffer: A peculiar or eccentric man; an old man; see *ancient.*

duffle: Cowboy's personal property; duds. See *plunder.*

dugout: A house built into a hillside and having a sod roof; also called a sod shanty. The only houses of the early settlers on the plains. They were warm in winter and like a furnace in summer.

dulce: Sweet; gentle. Spanish.

dumped: Thrown from a bucking horse; piled; spilled; bit the dust; see *chewed dirt.*

dun: A tan or dull-brown horse; also called a "buckskin."

dust: To go in a hurry. See *drag it.* To fog; also, gold-dust, gold or money.

dust front and back: Shoot through and through.

dutch courage: Whiskey or guns; anything used to bolster timorous nerves; a substitute for guts.

dutch oven: A deep, cast-iron skillet with legs and a flanged lid. This pot of "oven" is adapted for open fire cooking as it can be placed on a bed of live coals and the rimmed cover heaped with them. Any kind of food may be cooked in the oven. A good-sized cow camp will have several large dutch ovens sizzling at the same time, the number depending upon the size of the outfit.

-E-

earmark: To cut the ear or ears of a critter with the owners brand or mark.

earmarks: Wartles, vents, slices. The *underbit* and *overbit.*

eat dirt: To be spilled from a salty bronc. See *chewed dirt* and *dumped.* Eat gravel.

eenie meany: A short, bowlegged cowpoke.

egg: Aig.

egg float: Strong coffee. See *creekful of coffee.*

elbow bender: An eater or drinker. "Each time that gent bends his elbow, his mouth flies open."

encina: Evergreen oak. Spanish.

epizootic: An epidemic of distemper peculiar to horses. A cowboy's diagnosis of an unknown ailment of self. "Guess I ketched a epizootic."

estancia: A cattle ranch. Spanish.

et a bite: Ate a light lunch. See *bait uh vittles.*

euchered: A card game term meaning, "washed-up."; beat; cheated; finagled; swindled. See *cold-deck* and *deal from the bottom.*

even deal: An even chance; a 50-50 break.

ewe-necked: A horse with a neck like an ewe; a scrawny, ugly, hollowed out neck. Opposite of "arched neck."

-F-

facer: A puzzle which puts one at wit's end or against a blank wall.

fan: To slap a horse with sombrero when riding him to make him buck.

fanning: The striking of a pistol hammer with the heel of the hand not holding gun. This is done by a gun *fanner;* see *gun hawk.*

fantail: A wild, unbroken horse. See *bangtail.*

faro: A gambling game. Very destructive to cowboy's bankroll.

feeders: Cattle being fed up for market.

feel fine as possums: In the pink of condition.

feel fit as a fiddle: As above with possums, it means to be in the pink of condition.

fellers: Fellows.

fence lifter: A hard rain; see *goose drownder* or *gully washer.*

fence rider: Cowboy who rides along fence watching for breaks.

Fence-row: The zig-zag, stiff-legged jumps of a bucking horse.

fevertick and blackleg: Diseases fatal to livestock. See *anthrax.*

fiddle-head: A very common, small desert plant.

figger: Figure.

finicky: Particular; hard to please. "She's a finicky gal!"

firewater: Whiskey. Indian origin. Pizen; tarantula juice; licker; panther sweat; Dutch courage; snake remedy; tea.

fish: Cowboy's name for a slicker.

fish or cut bait: Stay in or get out; back up your big talk.

fist and skull: A hand-to-hand encounter. See *dog fight.*

flannel mouth: A braggart; a loud talker.

flat: A level stretch of country; prairie; plains; also, without funds; broke.

flea bitten: A white or gray horse flecked with tiny bay or sorrel dots; moth-eaten.

flunky: A roustabout; helper; dirt cuffer; see *swamper.*

fog: To shoot: to leave in a hurry; see *dust: drag it: light a shuck: light out: drift.*

fold up: To buck; to collapse.

foofaraw: To joke; to josh; to rib; to rawhide; to hooraw; horseplay; to kid.

fool hoe man: A dirt farmer; plow chaser; churn twister; sod buster; nester; squatter; see *cornfed granger.*

fore foot: To rope the front feet of an animal; to front-foot.

foreman: The immediate boss of the cowboys. The cowboy, like anyone else, does not relish two bosses. He will take orders from either foreman or owner but resents it when they both butt in.

forker: Mounted his horse; climbed aboard; straddled.

forty-five: The calibre of a gun; see *gun.* There is also a gun known as a forty-four; these guns were also called "forty-some-odd."

founder: To make a horse ill by over feeding.

fourflusher: A pretender; a bluffer; a braggart. See *tin-horn.*

fracas: Fracus: brawl; fight; ruckus; see *dogfight* and *difficulty.*

freeze!: Don't move!; hold it!

fried shirt: A stiff shirt; dress shirt; see, *boiled shirt.*

frijoles: Beans. Sometimes called "Mexican bread." "Free-holies."

frisky: Active; spry; playful. (Man or animal.) See *zipper.*

from hell to Halifax: A complete coverage of territory.

frying size: A youth; boy; younker; yonker. See *button.*

fuego: Fire. Spanish.

fuerte: A fort; strong; stout. Spanish.

full-rigged: A saddle with double cinches; double-barreled saddle; Miles City rig.

full-stamped: A saddle stamped with fancy designs.

fully dressed: Wearing six-gun and Winchester, ready to go places.

furriners: People from beyond the cow country; see *tenderfoot.*

fuzz tails: Mustangs or wild range horses; fantails; broomies; fuzzies; broncs. See *bang tails.*

-G-

gaff: The spur. Galves (plural). See *spurs.*

gal: Girl; filly; heifer; see *sage hen.*

gallery: Veranda; porch; wooden or iron awning.

gallin': Courting a girl; makin' calf's eyes. See *callin'.*

game: Without fear. To "be game" is to be gutty or courageous.

gambrel stick: A stick used to spread apart the hind legs of a butchered critter.

ganted-up: Tired out; thin or lean from fasting; showing signs of hard riding. From the adjective "gaunt," meaning "thin."

gazabo: A wise fellow; a smart aleck; a wiseacre. "Thet gazabo shore figgers he's some pumpkins!"

geared-up: A horse all saddled and bridled, ready to go.

geed up: Tuned up; ready; all set for fun, fight or frolic; see *skeed up* from whis-*skied*-up.

gelding: A horse which has been castrated. Horses showing poor stock are castrated to prevent breeding.

gent: Contraction of gentleman. Used derisively or in a very broad sense in referring to a man. See *man.*

Geronimo: A noted Apache chief, responsible for many killings.

get: To kill; rub-out; dry-gulch; pecos; ambush; bushwhack.

get strung out: To get set; all read; wised-up.

get the bulge: To gain an advantage over another.

get the drop: To be first in drawing the six-shooter. Very important in an encounter. There is a self explanatory saying in the west: "Slow draw, quick death."

get their hackles up: To become angry; peeved. See *on the prod.*

gigged: Spurred. See *comb: rake: rowel.*

Gila: An Arizona river flowing east to west, pronounced "heela."

Gila monster: A poisonous lizard native to Arizona and New Mexico.

girt: Girth; cinch; cincha; belly-strap; belly-band. A part of saddle rigging. See *cinch.*

give 'im the gaff: Spur him. See *rake: comb; rowel.*

glaum: To grab; snatch; seize forcibly.

goat: Term applied to a scrubby horse; a small, runty horse.

go belly up: To quit; take out. See *rabbited and coyoted.*

go clean: Go without blame; without taint.

go haywire: To miscarry; to go askew or awry.

goldarnia: Cowboy's version of "gardenia."

goose drownder: A torrential rain; cloudburst; a fence-lifter; snipe-bogger; see *gully-washer.*

goosy: Nervous; touch; jittery; ironically called "proud."

got a hen on: Have something planned.

got his wind up: Became angry. See *get their hackles up.*

gouged: Spurred; raked; roweled; gigged. Raking spurs along horses' sides. See *comb.*

grabbing leather: Pulling leather. Hanging on to horn or saddle to avoid being thrown from bucking horse. See *Leather.*

granger: A farmer. See *fool hoe man.*

grappling irons: Spurs; galves.

grass cutter: Cowboy term for a horse; a hayburner.

grass-bellied: Stuffed; full of; lousy with. "He was a grass-bellied with dinero."

grazing land: The range where cattle feed. May be owned, leased or preempted.

graveyard shift: The midnight shift of the night herder.

greaser: A Southwestern expression used to denote a Mexican. Also, Cholo; Spick; spik; Mex. See *chili eater.*

greasewood: A desert bus, also known as Creosote bush. Grows to twelve feet in height.

greener: A tenderfoot; newcomer; greenhorn. See Pilgrim.

green horse: A horse untrained for work with cattle. Also, an unbroken horse. See *break out a rough one.*

greybacks: Lice; ticks; any vermin; see *lice as big as chili beans.*

gringo: A name given to U.S. citizens by Mexicans.

ground tied: Letting the bridle reins trail on the ground in order to picket horse.

grub: Food; chuck; chow; duff; vittles. See *bait.*

grub-line rider: A moocher in cow camps and on ranches; a tramp; a saddle-bum. See *chuckline rider: saddle tramp.*

grub pile: Cooked food ready for eating. See *elbow bending: bait.*

grub stake: To outfit or provision another person for some purpose; also, money held in reserve for an emergency.

grullo: A horse; gruller. From Spanish "grulla" meaning a crane.

G-string: jee-string; A sort of dress worn by Indians before they became civilized.

guerrilla: An irregular warfare, carried on by roving bands. See *bushwhacker.*

gulch: A rugged, narrow gorge or ravine. See *canyon.*

gully: A small ravine worn by flooding water; a small dry stream bed; a draw; see *arroyo.*

gully-washer: A heavy downpour; see *goose-drownder.*

gumption: Grit; knowledge; common sense; "gumptious."

gun: pisto: revolver; derringer; artillery; hardware; six-gun; six-shooter; forty-four; forty-five; .45; forty-some-odd; Colt; S&W; Smith and Wesson; iron; shootin' iron; talkin' iron; dooey; dewey; cedar; smoke-pole; smoke-wagon; cutter; stinger; peacemaker; equalizer; fanner; hog-leg; hawg-laig; lead pusher.

gun fighter: A gent who settles his arguments with guns.

gun-hawk: A gun artist; one adept with guns; a gun-slick.

gun him!: Shoot him!

gunner: A wielder of firearms; a gun fighter.

gun slick: a gun-hawk.

gun-tipper: One who shoots through the open end of a swiveled hoster without drawing his gun.

gut hooks: Spurs; galves; grappling irons; see *spurs.*

gut kinker: A tornadic, bucking horse; a "gut-twister." The bronc snapper always gets plenty shaken up, hence the expression.

gut shoot: To shoot a man in his mid-section. Very effective.

gutty: Brave; nervy; without fear. See *game.*

-H-

hacienda: A Mexican plantation or ranch.

hack: A buggy, cart of other light vehicle; see *buckboard.*

hackamore: A bitless bridle made from rope, rawhide thongs or leather straps. Used frequently on unbroken horses, pack animals, etc.

hair bounty: Reward for a man's capture. Derived from custom of Indians on the warpath who removed the victim's hair by scalping.

hair brand: A temporary brand used by cattle thieves, made by pulling or cutting the hair from critter's hide into the desired pattern; a brand not burned into hide and which would soon grow over.

hair rope: A reata braided from hair. Extremely strong and flexible.

hair trigger: A trigger filed so as to discharge gun by a very slight pressure. The catches and trigger springs are especially treated; also means a person with a quick temper or one on edge. "The gent there has a hair trigger temper."

hammer-head: A horse with a blocky, ugly head; a stubborn horse or person.

ham string: To cripple.

hand: A cowboy; see *man.*

hang and rattle: Keep trying; persevere.

hang his hide on the fence: To expose; show-up.

hanker: To desire something to pine; see *hone.*

ha'nt: Haunt; a ghost; apparition; also, a contraction of has not.

hard boiled hat: A stiff hat; derby. Disliked by cowboys.

hard money: Coin as opposed to currency. See *dinero.*

hard mouthed: Not sensible to bridle signals; headstrong; willful; obstinate; see *cold-jawed.*

hard tails: Mules; rat-tails.

hardware: Revolvers. See *gun.*

hasher: A waitress; term also applied to the ranch or camp cook; see *biscuit shooter.*

hatful: Plenty; a quantity of anything. See *scads: slather: Hell's slew.*

haul yo're freight: Beat it!; a command to leave.

hawg's leg: See *gun.*

hawss: Horse; nag; cayuse; pinto; mount; gelding; mare; bronc; hoss; caballo (Spanish); hayburner; see *grass cutter.*

hayburner: Cowboy term for a horse; see *hawss.*

haze: To push or herd cattle or horses; to urge them forward. Animals are sometimes "hazed" when not actually driven, the idea being to get them from one spot to another by a "worrying" or "jockeying" process.

headin' fer th' last round-up: Dying; cashing-in; crossing over; bucking out; curling up; goin' over the range; taking the long trail; the big jump; see *cash-in.*

head taster: Ranch foreman; auger; ramrod; see *boss.*

heap walk man: Indian term for soldiers of infantry branch of service.

hear the owl hoot: Ride the night trail; follow outlawry. See Owlhoot; Hoot owler.

heel: To snag or rope an animal by the hind feet.

heeled: Prepared for any emergency; to carry a gun. Some cowboys declare they "feel downright naked, lessen they're heeled." See *gun.*

heifer brand: The arm ribbon or mark on a man at a dance who is impersonating a girl. This adds another heifer to the herd and gals are still sometimes scarce in parts of the west. See *baile* and *shindig.*

heifer dust: Bull Durham smoking tobacco. See *makin's.*

hell fer leather: Fast; "a-cootin'"; hell-bent-for-'lection.

hellin' around: Raising Cain; seeking sport, fight, fun or frolic.

hellion: A bad-un; a salty man or beast.

hell's catoot: Cowboy exclamation of surprise or dismay.

Hell's slew: A whole lot; a heap; see *hatful.*

hell wind: A tornado; cyclone.

hello!: 'Lo!

hemp: The lariat; rope; string; Manilla: lasso; lass' rope; twine; catgut; whale line; reata; see **riata: lariat.**

hemp fever: A hanging; one end of a rope around the neck and the other end over a limb. See **necktie party:** *Cottonwood fruit.*

hemp necktie: The hanging rope.

hen fruit stir: "Yes, sir! Pancakes with eggs in 'em, I Gawd!"

hen roost stuff: Booty obtained by petty thieving.

he'p: Contraction of "help."

herd: A number of horses, cattle or other animals. Also, the act of keeping them together.

hemana: Sister. Spanish.

hermano: Brother. Spanish.

hidalgo: Nobleman. Spanish.

hide: To whip. See *laying on the leather.*

hide-out: Place of concealment; refuge; hideaway.

highgraded: Stolen; swiped.

high-handed: Without regard for other's feelings; high an' mighty.

high lonesome: A prolonged spree; drunk as a hoot owl.

high roller: A horse that jumps far off the ground when bucking.

high tail: To hurry along; to depart; to beat it.

high tailed it: Ran away rapidly; see **vamoose.**

hi heits: Comanche Indian term meaning, "Howdy?" or "How are you?"

hisself: Himself.

h'ist one: To take a drink, especially at the bar.

hit a lick: An attempt to do something. "He never hit a lick in years."

hit the breeze - the grit - the trail - the turf: To travel; go.

hobble: The act of placing "hobbles" on a horse.

hobbles: Fetters around a horse's front feet to prevent wandering. Same as hopples. See *side-lined him.*

hog back: A ridge of hills or mountains; also, a horse with a prominent backbone; a razor-back.

hoggin' strings: Short lengths of rope or rawhide thongs used by cowboys in "hog-tying" or roping a critter's feet. See *piggin' strings.*

hog-leg: An Army Colt; now refers to any heavy pistol. See *gun.*

hog skin: A derisive term applied to an eastern saddle; also called "kidney-pad."

hokey-pokey: Chemical which violently agitates an animal.

hole up: The act of hiding out; to prepare against bad weather. "I allus lay in a supply of grub an' hole up fer th' winter."

hombre: Man. Spanish term widely used in Southwest.

home guard: The derisive name for a cowboy who sticks to his mother's apron strings and never strays far from his home range; a pampered son.

homely phizog: A homely face.

honda: The eye braided into the end of a reata through which the loop is formed. This is sometimes an oval-shaped iron ring called a "honda ring." "Headed for the honda end of the rope," means that a man is heading for a reckoning, or the end.

hone: To want; to desire greatly; pine for; long. See *hanker.*

honkatonk: A house of hilarity in the tenderloin or red-light district; all cow towns have 'em.

hooden: A cabin used by cowboys in bad weather.

hoodlum wagon: Wagon used to haul supplies during round-up.

hook-up: To join forces; associate with; form a partnership.

hooks: Spurs; sometimes refers to the hands.

hooraw: To joke; tease; lead on; rib; see *foofaraw.*

horsing around: The awkward play of cowboys. *Noorawing.*

hoot owler: An outlaw; see *owl hoot: long rider: long rope.*

hornin' in": Butting in; meddling; interfering.

horn spread: Width of a cow's horns from tip to tip.

horse: A nag; hoss; hawse; skate; caballo; hayburner; grasscutter; pinto; cayuse; bronc; mustang; see *hawss: bangtail: fuzztail.*

Horse-pistol: A heavy pistol. See *gun.*

Horse wrangler: Cowboy who takes care of remuda.

hoss: Contraction of horse.

hot blood: A Thoroughbred horse. See *cold blood.*

hospital cattle: Weak cattle.

hot foot: To hurry.

hot roll: Bedding. See *soogan.*

how come?: How does or did it happen?

howdedo: A mess; dilemma; a fix. "A fine howdedo!"

hull: A saddle; kak; kack; tree; trough; wood; leather. Hull is from "husk," meaning covering or outer skin.

hundred-and-eleven's: 111's; Rowel marks on a horse's flank.

hung his head: Bogged his head. Humped his back.

hunker: To squat down on the hams. The cowboy is in typical posture off his horse when sitting on his heels.

hunky-dory: O.K.; just right; perfect.

hunt their holes: Go into hiding. See *hole up.*

hurricane deck: The saddle. "On the hurricane deck of a bronc."

hyar: Here.

-I-

idiota: Idiot. Spanish.

idjut: The way a cowboy says "idiot."

I don't hold tuh th' idear: I have a different opinion.

in cahoots with: In alliance with; partners; pards; pardners; podners. See *hook up.*

Indian fire: A small dry-wood fire.

Indio: Indian. Spanish.

injun: Indian. (Cowboy)

inta: Into.

iron: The branding iron; also, a pistol or "shootin' iron." See *gun.*

ironwood: An Arizona tree with strong, hard wood and thorny twigs. Grows to eighteen feet.

I.T.: Indian Territory, now included in the state of Oklahoma.

itching feet: Wanderlust; a yen to travel.

ivories: Poker chips; also refers to a piano; in the singular means "soap."

-J-

jack: Money. See *dinero* and *hard-money.* Also a contraction of "jackrabbit," the long-eared, fleet-footed bunny of the plains.

jackpot: A poker term; also, trouble or difficulty; a jam.

jagged: Drunk. See *tanked.*

jail aimed: Headed for trouble; said of a reckless, troublesome gent.

jamboree: A big time; blow-out; celebration; drinking party; dance or fight. See *hellin' around: stampede.*

jaquima: Jakama; a hackamore rope.

jar: "He left with a jar," i.e. quickly or hurriedly.

jasper: A smart aleck; a wiseacre. See *man.*

java: Coffee; see *Arbuckle; barefoot coffee.*

J.B.: A hat. Contraction of John B. Stetson. A XXXX Beaver; sombrero; conk cover.

jefe: Chief; leader. Spanish.

jerk line: A single, long leather line used to control two or more teams hitched to the same vehicle.

jerky: Dried or "jerked" beef: meat cut into thin strips and dried in the sun. Very nourishing.

jigger: An insignificant person. See *man.*

jigeroo: A salty gent; a tough 'un; see *curly wolf.*

jig step: Fancy capers.

Jim Crow: Outfit: A small ranch; a dilapidated place.

jimson weed: The poisonous thornapple.

jingler: The horse wrangler.

jobbed: Teased; ribbed; see *hooraw: foofaraw.*

jockey box: A box at the side of a wagon.

jog: The slow gait of a horse, between a walk and a trot: to turn aside; a bend or turn in the trail.

John B.: See *J.B.*

Joshua Trees: The yucca palm. These trees from fantastic shapes and at a distance are often mistaken for a man or animals even by the natives. They grow to thirty feet.

jug: A jail; calaboose; hoosegow; carcel; see *juzgado.*

jughead: A boneheaded horse; a blocky-headed horse; also used in connection with a half-baked human.

Juice: To milk a cow; to "pail" or "pump" a cow. See *pail.*

jumping bean: A Mexican bean in which a worm makes it home. When the worm wiggles, the bean jumps. Sold in curio stores along the border.

june along: To travel leisurely and steadily. See *ooze along.*

june around: To wander about aimlessly.

juniper tree: An evergreen shrub or tree, usually low and spreading.

Justins: A popular brand of handmade cowboy boots made in Fort Worth, Texas, sometimes running into important money.

juzgado: A jail; jug; calaboose; hoosegow; carcel; cuartel. "Hoosegow" comes from the Spanish word "juzgado," meaning court or tribunal. Adapted to mean "jail."

-K-

kaboodle: The whole; whole lot.

kak: Kack; a saddle; leather; see *hull.*

kayack boxes: Dunnage boxes; baskets or boxes lashed to pack saddles, usually in pairs, for carrying supplies. Also spelled *kyack.*

kepi: A cap.

ketch dog: A dog, usually a mongrel of indefinite origin, used in some sections of the west to aid cowboys in cornering wily, fleet-footed steers. A good ketch dog must be clever, fast and unafraid. He goes after the steer front or rear, often seizing its tender nose and throwing the animal. Due to the mauling, kicking and pawing received from the cattle, the life a a ketch dog is fast but short.

ketched: Caught. "I shore ketched hell fer soapin' Shorty's boot soles."

kettle: To buck; too scare.

kibosh: The finishing touches. "I'll put the kibosh on it, pronto!"

kick over the traces: To rebel against anything. From the action of a team of horses which refuse to pull a load.

kidney pad: A saddle used for pleasure riding. See *hog skin.*

killer: Just what the word implies. May be a man, horse, steer or bull.

kill your own snake: Do your own fighting.

kinky pony: A hard bucking bronc.

kiss the book: Tell the absolute, unvarnished truth.

knob-headed hoss: A stubby-headed horse. See *jug head* and *hammerhead.*

knocked cow-west: Knocked out; reduced to an unconscious state; knocked galley-west; knocked sky-west.

knuckle down: Submit to a stronger person or a stronger will; knuckle under.

kow-tow: To pay homage to; bow and scrape.

kyack boxes: See *kayack boxes.*

-L-

ladron: Thief; robber; highwayman. Spanish.

ladronera: A den of robbers; a hangout. Spanish.

lallygag: To loaf around; to idle; also, idle talk.

lambast: To hit or strike.

lane: A narrow road leading between two points on a ranch.

lariat: The lasso; lass' rope; rope; saddle rope; string; hemp; twine; reata; riata; catgut; whale line. The rope used by cowboys to catch and hold cattle and horses. A very important item of equipment. The whale line rope used east of the mountains will average thirty-five feet in length, while the horse-hair "reata" in use in California, Oregon and Nevada will run up to sixty feet. See *California rigging: dab: reata: honda.*

larrupin': Very good; tasty. Also refers to a whipping.

lass' rope: The lariat.

latigo: Strips of rawhide or leather used for lacing on a saddle girth.

laying on the leather: Spanking with a pair of chaps.

layout: The ranch as a whole; a gambling outfit; faro layout.

lawman: A representative of the law; sheriff, marshal, etc.

law trail: On the side of the law; law enforcer; opposed to *outlaw* or *hoot owler.*

lead pizen: Quick death; bullets. "He ketched a dose of lead pizen."

lead thrower: A six-gun or one who uses it; a lead-pusher; *gun.*

leary: Wary; suspicious; uncertain. "I'm leary of thet hombre."

leastwise: At least.

leather: The saddle. See *hull.* Leather is a very important item of the cowboy's equipment. His chaps, boots, belt and holster, gloves, saddle, bridle and quirt are of leather as well as wristlets and jacket when he rides in brush. The dally man uses a leather reata. See *batwing chaps.*

leppy: An orphaned or deserted calf; see *dogie.*

le's: Let us.

Levis: A popular brand of overalls worn by cowboys, made by Levi Strauss of San Francisco. The cowboy wears overalls without bibs and so distinguishes himself from the dirt farmer who wears the bib variety.

lice as big a chili beans: You find them like this along the border and in Mexico. See **greybacks.**

lick: Syrup; molasses.

licker: Whiskey; likker.

lid: The hat; see *sombrero: J.B.*

life preserver: Six-shooter; see *gun.*

light and eat: Cow country invitation to stop for a meal.

light out: Go; leave; see *drift* and *dust.*

like wild steers headin' yonderly: Every which way.

likewise: Also.

limber-back bronc: A hard bucker.

line: A lasso; hemp; string; rope; see *lariat: reata.*

line-back: A dun horse with black stripe running from withers to base of tail. Sometimes runs over shoulders and down forelegs.

line boss: The ranch foreman; segundo. See *boss.*

line camp: A camp out on the range used as a base from which to work. A subsidiary of home ranch. See *cow camp.*

lined out: Rode out.

lint-back: A cotton picker.

lingo: Language; jargon.

lion "scratch": Scratches on trees made by a mountain lion.

llano: A plain. Spanish.

lobo: A wolf. Spanish. Unlike the sneaky coyote, the lobo is strong and fierce. Usually hunts in packs and can pull down a full-grown steer.

locked horns: Engaged in physical combat. The fighting steer gave us this expression.

locked-spurs: Spurs with rowels fastened so they will not turn. In surcingle riding, the locked rowels are hooked in surcingle to aid rider in retaining seat.

locoed: Crazy or demented. Refers to stock or men. The locoweed plant, growing in Southwest, when eaten by livestock causes a form of insanity.

long box: A coffin; wooden kimono; wooden overcoat.

long-haired pard: A wife.

Longhorn: A native of Texas; a Texican; Tejano. Also, the cattle raised in Texas which had an enormous horn spread.

long rider: One who rides outside the law; a bandit; an owl hooter; see *outlaw.*

long rope artist: A cattle rustler or horse thief so called because of his long reach in snaring stock other than his own. See *wide loop.*

long sleep: Death; the end of the trail; over the ridge. See *headin' fer the last round-up: cash in.*

looked jake: In the pink of condition.

look-see: Take a look; investigate.

loop: The noose of a lariat. "To shake out a loop" or "build a loop" means to form a loop in the lariat before throwing. See *blocker loop: dab: honda: lariat.*

lope: The easy gait of a horse comparable to a canter or loafing gallop so frequently made use of by ponies in western states.

loosen him!: Encouragement to a horse to throw the rider.

loose herd: To herd loosely, permitting animals to graze.

lunch hooks: The hands; grub hooks; hooks; flippers.

-M-

make a pass: The attempt of one person to strike another.

making medicine: To plan or discuss anything; to mix medicine. Adopted from the Indian. See *pow-wow: wau-wau.*

makin's: A sack of tobacco and cigarette papers. See *build a quirly.* Also called Durham and Bull. See *heifer dust.*

man: Hombre; gent; jasper; jigger; feller; hand; hairpin; screw; cow hand; cow nurse; 'poke or cowpoke; cow waddy; cowpuncher; 'puncher; ranny; rannihan; ranahan; buster; bronc buster; bronc breaker; bronc chouser; bronc peeler; bronc snapper; bronc stomper; bronc twister; bronc wrangler; horse wrangler; dude wrangler; wrangler; twister; peeler; waddie; waddy; and plain old cowboy.

mama: Mamma. Spanish.

mammy: A cow with suckling calf. See *wet stuff.*

mañana: Tomorrow. Sp. Mexico is called the land of mañana.

manger: To visit the manger is to surreptitiously take a drink, especially at a cowboy dance.

man-talk: Big talk; bluffing; boisterous declaration.

marco: A branding iron. Spanish.

mare: A female horse, young or old; a stock horse. Called a filly when young.

marijuana: Marijuanna; a narcotic plant growing in Mexico and along the border. Produces a form of mild insanity when smoked over a period of time.

marker: A critter easily recognized by odd markings.

martingale: A check rein used to hold down a horse's head and to prevent tossing of head.

maverick: An unbranded critter. Many big ranches were started by owners riding the range and branding mavericks. The word "maverick: is said to have originated from the operations of one John Maverick of Texas who made a business of marking all unbranded critters with his brand. There is also another story to the effect that he branded nothing, hence the name, "maverick."

maybeso: Perhaps; may be; it is possible.

Mc Carthies: Hair ropes.

mebbe: Same as *maybeso.*

mecate: A hair rope. Spanish.

medicine: Information. See *making medicine.* Also used in some localities in referring to whiskey. See *snake remedy.*

mesa: A flat-topped elevation. Spanish word meaning "table."

mequit: A thorny tree with leaves like those of a pepper tree, found alone or in clumps. Grows to eighteen feet. Spanish, mesquite.

Mexican: Bean-eater; chola; greaser; shuck; spic; spick; chili-eater.

Mexican iron: rawhide.

Mexican serge: Overalls.

Mexican strawberries: Beans.

middle of evening: Late afternoon.

millin' around a jug: A drinking party; visit the manger; see *manger* and *tanked.*

mind: Attention. "I don't pay him no mind."

mío: My; mine. Spanish.

misdoubt: Don't think so; disbelief; doubt.

missed his cue: Failed to understand; didn't savvy.

mix medicine: Same as *make medicine.*

mochila: Knapsack; bed-roll.

mocho: Dehorned. Spanish.

mockeys: Wild mares. (Arizona)

monte: A gambling, card game, popular along Mexican border.

morrel: The nose bag; feeding bag for horses and mules. (Arizona)

mosey: To go slowly; ooze along. See *amble along: june along.*

mount: A horse; nag. See *horse: cayuse: pinto.*

mount money: A rodeo term; usually $5.00 for each horse or critter forked by a cowboy; hence, puny reward; small time change; hen roost stuff.

mosshead: A very old steer.

moss horn: An old steer with scaly horns; a moss back.

motte: A thicket.

muchacha: Girl **muchacho:** Boy. Spanish.

mujer: Woman. Spanish.

muley: Without horns; a breed of cattle. Also called "mooley."

muley saddle: A saddle without horns.

mustang: A wild or semi-broken pony of the Southwestern states; fuzztail; broomtail.

mustang runners: Men who make a business of building traps and catching mustangs and wild horses, which are later broken and sold.

muy bueno: Very good. *Muy malo:* Very bad.

muy pronto: Very quick. Spanish.

-N-

nada: Nothing. Spanish.

nary: None; not.

nary a thing: Nothing at all.

neckerchief: A large handkerchief of silk or cotton worn about the cowboy's neck for protection against dust and sun. No cowboy's outfit is complete without a gaudy neckerchief.

neck o' the woods: A particular section; locals. "Jest like it is in my neck o' the woods."

necktie party: A hanging; lynching. See *hemp fever* and *cottonwood fruit.*

ne'mind: Never mind.

nester: One who files on, buys or lives on a piece of land and operates it as a farm; an invader of the range. See *squat: cornfed granger* and *fool hoe man.*

nicker of a horse: The cry, neigh or whinny of a horse.

nigh horse: The horse nearest the driver of a team; the left-hand horse. The *off horse* is the one on the right.

night guard: The night herder of cattle. The night shift is divided into several "tricks" of usually two hours each.

night hawk: The night horse wrangler. The *remuda* or horse herd is looked after by the day wrangler and the night hawk, neither of whom have anything to do with the cattle.

nine ways from the jack: Every which way; all over.

nino: Baby. Spanish.

no medicine: No dope; no information.

not a red: Without a cent; flat broke; financially defunct.

notch 'im off: Kill him; add another notch to the butt of the six-gun; a record of killings.

nòtch in his tail: Said of a horse that has killed a man.

not what it's cracked up to be: Something misrepresented.

not worth a whoop: Without value. "His word's not worth a whoop."

nubbin': The saddle horn. The favorite hold of inexperienced riders when horse bucks. Called "pulling leather"; "grabbing the nubbin, the post or the apple"; see *grabbing leather.*

-O-

off 'n th' deep end: In dire trouble; no last resort.

oiled: Drunk; intoxicated on "panthersweat." See *tanked: skeed-up.*

oiler: A derisive name applied to a Mexican; greaser; chili eater; cholo. See *Mexican.*

oily bronc: A wily bronc: one with plenty of life or meanness.

O.K.: Oklahoma killer; a sign or agreement.

Oklahoma rain: A sandstorm.

old lady: The cook; Susie; Sarah; old woman; see *cookie.*

onct: Once.

one horse outfit: A small outfit; a "greasy-sack" outfit.

on shank's mare: Afoot: walking; unhorsed.

on the injun list: On the blacklist; having no liquor credit. There is a federal law against selling liquor to Indians.

on the prod: Very angry; all steamed up; hunting trouble; peeved; on the peck.

on the prowl: Combing territory after round-up to pick up additional strays or "hid-out" cattle.

on tick: On credit.

on trigger: Nervous; flighty; "on trigger's edge."

Onwind: When a horse starts bucking he "onwinds." See *unwind.*

ooze along: To move slowly. See *june along: mosey along.*

orejano: An unclaimed or unbranded animal; one with an unreadable or unfamiliar brand. "Orejano" as used in California, Oregon and Nevada is equivalent to "slick-ear" used in other sections of the west. See *California rigging.*

ornery: Mean; of no account. Refers to men or animals.

oro: Gold. Spanish.

outfit: The cowboy's equipment, such as saddle, bridle, horse, hen skin (saddle blanket), lariat, spurs, chaps, etc. Word also used in referring to some particular ranch or organization.

outlaw: An untameable or unbreakable horse or one that has become vicious through improper handling; also, a robber, bandit, highwayman, hoot-owler.

outrider: A cowboy whose duty it is to locate scattered groups of cattle and "bunch" them. He also notes condition of grass and water, moves cattle back from border of range, keeps an eye peeled for rustlers and wolves.

overbit: A method of car marking, either ear being cut. See *underbit: steeple fork: swallow fork.*

owl-headed horse: A wise or stubborn horse.

owlhoot: Outside the law.

owlhoot buckeroo: An outlaw cowboy.

owlhooter: One who rides the outlaw trail; see *outlaw: long rider: hootowler: long rope artist.*

-P-

pack: To carry, as a gun. The cowboy always "packs" his gun or his bed-roll; he never "carries" it. Also, a bundle of the cowboy's necessities, such as provisions, slicker, etc.

packed his irons: Carried his guns; went armed. See *heeled.*

packer: The leader of pack animals; man in charge of them.

pack horse or **pack mule:** Animal used in carrying supplies or equipment over difficult trail.

packing plenty taller: Fat; in good condition.

pack rat: A species of rat infesting the west. This animal carries away shiny objects and stores them in nest. Occasionally their dens are veritable storehouses of valuables, especially if there are houses nearby.

pack stock: Animals used in packing luggage.

padre: Father; priest. Spanish.

pail: To milk or "pump" a cow. See *juice.*

paint horse: A piebald pony; a pony splotched with colors. *Pinto.*

palaver: Talk. See *pow wow* and *wau-wau.*

pan: Bread; food. Spanish.

panhandle: To beg; an historical section of Texas. Also, Oklahoma.

panniers: Pack bags or baskets. They usually come in pairs. See *alforja* and *kayack boxes.*

panther sweat: Whiskey; pizen; firewater; see *snake remedy.*

parada: The main herd. From Spanish word meaning parade. (Used in California, Oregon and Nevada.)

pard: Same as partner. The cowboy might say pardner.

pasear: To walk; a trip; journey. Spanish.

passel: Many; several; a crowd. "A passel of 'em rod in."

pass in his chips: To die.

paunches full of good grass and water: Livestock in prime condition.

peak: To turn or pinch the brim of the sombrero into a point. The cowboy always peaks the wide brim of his hat.

Pecos: A river in New Mexico and western Texas along which much meaty history has been made. Also, a term used in referring to the dumping of a man's body into a stream after he has be shot from ambush.

Pecos Bill: A legendary liar from west Texas.

peeler: The rider of wild horses; twister; snapper. See *man.*

peon: A Mexican laborer.

peso: The Mexican dollar. Adopted along the border and applied to United States money.

picayunish: Very particular; complaining; fretful.

piebald: Spotted. See *calico: paint horse* and *pinto.*

pie-eyed: Drunk; soused; stiff; lit; lickered-up. See *tanked.*

piggin' string: A short length of rope or rawhide thong used in tying the feed of a critter after it is roped. See *hoggin' string.*

pilgrim: A tenderfoot; newcomer; dude; greenhorn; greener; maverick; one unfamiliar with ranch life.

pill roller: A doctor: M.D. See *sawbones.*

pilot of the round-up wagon: The guide on round-up who leads the way to the next campground.

pimienta: Pepper. Spanish.

pincushion: The fish-hook cactus. An edible plant growing two inches high.

pin-eared: The sharp, pointed ears of a horse.

pinon: The dwarfed or stunted pine tree.

pinto: A spotted horse. See *paint horse: piebald: calico.*

pious idea: A very good idea.

pirooting: Pirouetting; the whirling about of a horse.

pistol: Artillery; hardware. See *gun.*

pistolo: Pistol. Spanish.

pistol-cutter: Something wonderful. "That gal is a pistol-cutter."

pitch: A card game; see *seven-up: solo: monte: stud: faro.*

pitching: Bucking; unwinding; onwinding; boiling over; uncorking. See *bogged his head: buck: ruck off.*

pizen: A contraction of poison. Anything bad; whiskey. See *snake remedy.*

plain trail: A clear, readable trail.

plant: To bury; hide; conceal. When a gent dies out west, he is "planted," not buried.

plata: Silver. Spanish.

plated: Shod.

played his string out: Died; finished; completed a job.

playing the coffee pot: Drinking coffee.

play injun: To feign death; to play 'possum; to imitate and Indian's wily tricks.

plenty wrinkles on his horns: Old; aged. Also applies to wisdom or shrewdness coming from age.

plow chaser: A farmer. See Churn twister: Cornfed granger: Fool hoe man: Nester: Sod buster.

plug: To shoot anyone; a broken-down horse; a plodder.

plugged: Shot.

plumb: Sure; all; total. "I'm plumb glad to see you."

plunder: A cowboy's personal effects; loot. See *dunnage.*

poco a poco: Little by little. Spanish.

point: To ride "point" is to lead or guide the moving herd, with a rider on either side of the herd. Point riders are always experienced top hands. See *swing rider* and *drag rider.*

'poke: Cowpoke; cowpuncher. See *man.* A "poke" is a bag.

polecat: A skunk. Applied to an odious, treacherous person.

pommel: The knob or horn of a saddle.

poncho: A waterproof square with an opening in the center to that it may be pulled over the head. Used in lieu of a slicker or "fish." Sometimes a blanket is used for the same purpose as a poncho. The arms are left free.

poor as a snake: Plenty lean; without tallow. Just the opposite of "packing plenty taller and pretty snuffy."

popped off: Spoke out of turn; made a bombastic statement.

posse: Band of men hurriedly organized for running down lawbreakers.

postage stamp: An eastern saddle.

potbelly: Distended middle; pot gutted; refers to either man or horse. See *dough belly: whey belly.*

pothole: Cavity or depression in rock. Some of these potholes are filled with water thirty feet deep with only a thin crust of earth on top and are therefore very dangerous. Usually found in the badlands.

pothook: A device for holding kettle over campfire or fireplace.

pot rassler: The dishwasher. See *bull cook: flunky: swamper.*

potro: A colt. Spanish.

pounding leather: Riding, especially hard riding.

Powerful: A great quantity; very much; "powerful glad" and "powerful sorry." "I'm powerful glad to see you." See *plumb.*

powerful-great sheriff: His nibs hisself, not a deputy.

pow-wow: A talk or discussion. See *making medicine: wau-wau.*

prairie: A level, unbroken sweep of country; the plains.

prairie coal: Dried cow dung. See *cow chips: buffalo chips.*

prairie dog: A burrowing rodent infesting the prairie country. Sometimes used for food in an emergency. See **dog town.**

prairie lawyers: Wolves.

prairie schooner: A canvas-covered wagon. The vehicle used by '49ers in crossing the plains.

praties: Potatoes; spuds; murphys.

prayer bones: Knees.

pretties: A fancy outfit. "Lots of pretties on his rig."

prickly pear: Cactus plant with prickly joints inserted upon each other. The Indian fig.

prime long twos: Two-year-old steers in good flesh, ready for market. See *yearling.*

prod pole: A long, metal-tipped pole used in prodding or punching cattle up a loading ramp into stock cars. The terms "cowpuncher" and "cowpoke" are derived from the use of the prod pole.

pronghorn: Antelope.

pronto!: Quickly!; hurry!; ándale! Spanish.

pueblo: A town; the communal dwellings of the Pueblo and Moqui Indians.

pulled a fast one: Put one over; ran a shenanigan.

pull leather: This expression comes from the rider of a bucking horse who seizes saddle horn to aid in keeping his seat; chokin' the horn; *grabbing leather:* grabbin' the nubbin.

pull your freight: A command to leave; vamoose; get out.

pull your horns: Back up; stop; eat mud; back down.

pulque: A very potent Mexican beverage distilled from cactus sap.

pumped a cow: Milked a cow. See *juice* and *pail a cow.*

pumpkin head: A numbskull; blockhead; nitwit.

pumpkin roller: A grumbler or agitator. A "pumpkin roller" is as popular in cow camp as smallpox.

pure McCoy: Real; genuine; "pure-D"; pure-quill.

put a crimp: Interfere; place an obstruction in the way of. "I'll put a crimp in his style, pronto!"

put the string on: To rope. See *dab his twine.*

-Q-

queer anything: To spoil a play; to obstruct.

querida: Dear; darling; sweetheart. Spanish.

querly: See *quirly* and *makin's.*

quien es?: Who is it? Spanish. The last words spoken by Bill the Kid before Pat Garrett rubbed him out.

quien sabe?: Who knows? Spanish.

que tiene?: Wht have you? or What is the matter? Spanish.

quirly: A cigarette. See *build a querly: makin's: heifer dust.*

Quirt: A short whip of braided rawhide with multiple-thong lash. See *cutting quirt.* To quirt is to whip. Also called *romal:* quisto. "Quisto-mal" is Spanish, means "hated."

quite some: Quite a bit.

-R-

rabbit: To quit when most needed; to run out. See *coyoted.*

racing gallop: The fast gait of a horse.

rack: To ride.

rafter brand: A brand with an inverted "V" placed over the letter, figure or symbol and called "rafter J", "rafter T", etc.

raid: The hostile invasion of another's property or premises.

raise the roof: A noisy celebration; raise Cain.

rake: Dragging the spurs along a horse's sides. See *comb: spur.*

ramble: Go along steadily; go about one's business.

rambunctious: Impulsive; careless of consequences. See *on the prod.*

ramrod: To boss anything; to "rod" anything; the head of a ranch. See *boss.*

ranch: An area of land devoted to raising cattle, horses or sheep. See *spread* and *outfit.*

rancher: Refers strictly to the man who owns the spread.

ranchero: Rancher. Spanish.

ranch house: The dwelling on the home ranch.

ranchmen: Employees and bosses of an outfit.

rancho: The ranch. Spanish.

range: The land being grazed by a rancher's stock.

range boss: The man in charge of a herd.

range branded: Stock roped and branded on the open range as opposed to corral branding.

range hog: A rancher or outfit who tries to corral choice water holes and does not play square with his neighbors.

rannihan: Ranahan; ranny; a top-hand. See *man.*

rannikaboo: A trick; subterfuge; joke; blarney.

ranniky: Skittish; wily; cagey; angry. See *on the prod.*

ranny: Contraction of *rannihan.* A top hand.

rat-tailed: A horse with a scraggly tail. A tail with few hairs.

rattled his hocks: Hurried; departed in a rush. See *dust.*

rattlesnake weed: A border weed. The Spanish golondrina.

raw bronc: A wild, unbroken horse. See *snuffy bronc.*

rawhide: Untanned or green leather from the hide of a cow or steer. The cowboy's substitute for nails, needles and string; known as Mexican iron. Rawhide has wide uses in the cattle country. To "rawhide" an animal or person is to whip it. The word also refers to baiting, teasing or ribbing anyone.

rawhide flapjacks: Tortillas, especially when old or tough.

reach: A command to elevate the hands. "Reach fer th' sky, hombre!"

reata: The lariat. More especially the sixty foot rawhide lasso adopted from the Mexican vaquero. See *lariat: rata* and *California rigging.*

reckon: To think; guess; the intent to do something. "I reckon I'll ramble."

red-eye: Whisky. See *pizen* and *snake remedy.*

reef: To spur. See *comb: rake; rowel.*

relief: Change of riders; change of herd guards.

rep: (representation) A cowboy whose duty it is to represent his employer at other ranches, especially at round-up time when he brands his employer's calves and delivers them to the home range. Also called a "stray" man. As verb, means to represent. "He was reppin' at Tate's for the Bar-X-Bar.

remuda: The band of saddle horses used by cowboys during round-up. See *cavvy.* In Montana-Wyoming no mares are allowed in the remuda. The horse wrangler is in charge.

remudera: The bell mare of the Spanish cavvyada or remuda. This aids horse wrangler or nighthawk in locating the horse herd. See *bell mare.*

renegade: Outlaw horse or man. See *outlaw.*

renig: To quit; back down. See *pull your horns.*

riata: The lariat; lasso; lass' rope; reata; rope; hemp; twine; string; maguey; whale line; catgut; saddle rope; line. See *lariat.*

rib: Urge on; bait; tease; influence.

ricoshay: Ricochet; glance away; deflect.

ride down a horse: Ride a horse to exhaustion.

rider: Cowboy working for a certain outfit. See *man.*

ride herd: To watch; to manage or herd cattle; to keep the cattle gathered together.

ride slick: To ride a critter without saddle or bridle.

ridge runner: A fleet-footed, wily horse or steer; a wild one frequenting the broken country.

riding gun sign: Looking for trouble.

riding sign: See **sign camp.**

rig: A vehicle, such as a buckboard. Also, saddle gear; cowboy's equipment.

riggin': Cowboy's paraphernalia. Same as rig.

rigging ring: The ring just below saddle horn to which latigos holding stirrup leathers in place are secured.

right smart: A quantity; a whole lot. "I think a right smart of that cayuse."

rim-fire cigar: An important cigar.

ringy: Angry; peevish; mad; ireful. See *on the prod.* "The cook was ringy that day."

rio: River; stream. Spanish.

rip snorter: A wild, reckless man or animal

road agent: A bandit; highwayman; robber of stage coaches; see *outlaw: hootowler.*

road brand: A temporary brand put on stock while being trail-herded from one point to another. See *trail brand.*

roaring ram: A braggart; blusterer; fourflusher.

rocking brand: A quarter-circle brand with ends up, having the letter, figure or symbol resting within curve. Called, Rocking R, Rocking M, etc.

rod: Ramrod; boss; auger. See *boss.* To "rod" an outfit is to boss it.

rode his hoss to a standstill: Retained seat in saddle until horse quit bucking.

Rodeo: The round-up. The term also applies to the western celebration also known as War-bonnets, Frontier Day Celebration, Reunion, Round-up. Of Spanish origin, pronounced "ro-day-o," but always "rode-e-o" by the cowboy. Contests and races between picked riders, ropers and bull-doggers make up the rodeo. Salty-oxen, the wild steers of the mountain country who rarely see man or horse, together with the most vicious and ornery of the gut-twisting outlaws are always on hand to test the riders' mettle. The wild cow is whooped out of a chute, chased, roped and 'juiced.' Riding the wild Brama Bull, calf roping, trick roping and steer riding are among the sports. In the activities of the rodeo, enviable records are often hung up by the woman riders.

roll a loop: Wave-like motion of a thrown rope. See *dab.*

romal: A quirt.

roman-nosed: A horse with a hooked nose.

rope: The lasso; also, the act of roping. See *dab: reata: riata: lariat.*

'rose to th' 'casion: Met a challenge; took command; accepted a dare.

rotgut: Bad whiskey; red-eye. See *snake remedy* and *pizen.*

rough: Wild; wolly; salty; snuffy; rough. See *rough string: curly wolf and salty.*

rough one: A semi-broken horse, always willing to buck; a member of the *rough string.*

rough shod: Without consideration of another's feelings. "Tate rode "rough shod" over all the ranchers in Apache county.

rough string: Each rider is assigned a "string" of ten or twelve horses from the remuda as his personal mounts during round-up, etc. The "rough string" are the bad animals of the outfit; outlaws and spoiled horses which fight and buck whenever mounted. These horses are usually assigned to the more skillful riders.

round-up: The gathering together of all the cattle on the range. Ranchers combine forces and drive the critters into a main herd, where they are sorted to various owners. Slick calves, identified as belonging to a particular outfit by the cows they follow, are ear-marked and branded. Round-ups are held during cool weather whenever possible, usually in spring and fall of the year. In some sections it is called "rodeo."

rowel: The spiked wheel of the spur. Also, the act of spurring or "roweling." To "curry him out." See *spur: rake: comb.*

rub out: To kill anyone.

ruck-off: Action of a horse when he commences to buck. See *boil over: uncork: onwind: unwind: bogged his head.*

rucus: Ruckus; rumpus; a fight; trouble. See *difficulty: dog fight: fracus.*

running iron: An iron or copper rod used for tracing brands; an emergency iron as distinguished from the set branding iron. A cinch rig, when heated and held by a pair of pliers, makes a good running iron. Years ago, in Texas, it was a serious offence to be caught with heat-blackened cinch rings, due to the activities of cattle rustlers using that device for running brands upon stolen cattle. In most western states possession of a running iron is illegal.

rurales: Mexican border police.

rustler: A cattle thief. The terms usually used are "Cattle Rustler" and "Horse Thief." Formerly referred to the wrangler or herder of the remuda. See *wrangler.*

-S-

sabe: Understand? Spanish. See *savvy.*

sacked 'em out: Tying a sack or saddle blanket over a horse's eyes so that he can be saddled more easily and then untying and flipping the sack about his head to get him accustomed to such things.

saddle: A hull; kak; kack; tree; wood; leather; snow-plow; hog trough; the hurricane deck. A single-rigged saddle (one cincha) is referred to as a center-fire and single-shot. (See *California rigging.*) There are five positions in which the cinch is set on the single-rigged saddle: centerfire, 5/6, 3/4, 7/8 and Spanish. By the different positions, the location of the cinch ring from the center toward the front of saddle, is determined. In the Spanish rig, the cinch ring is directly below the horn.

In the double-rig or double cincha saddle the front cinch-ring is placed the same as in the Spanish rig with the back ring directly beneath the cantle. There is also the three in one rig which has the combined qualities of the single and double-rigged saddles.

Saddle weights vary from 28 to 45 pounds, according to quality. Current prices run from $30.00 up. A full-stamped, full-rigged, silver mounted saddle will sell for $500.00, the sky being the limit when you order a fancy kak. In mountainous country breast straps and breeching are added to saddle rigging.

saddlebags: Leather bags carried behind cantle of saddle, useful in packing cowboy's plunder. See *alforja.*

saddle blanket: A small blanket placed between the saddle and the horse's back to protect the latter. Also called "pancake," "flap-jack" and "hen-skin." These come in plain colors and in ornate designs. In the south the Navajo is popular and is sold be the pound. A single blanket will weigh three pounds and a double one, six pounds. Saddle pads, twenty-four inches square, are also used in protecting the horse's back from saddle chafing.

saddle boot: Scabbard for carbine, Winchester or other long gun, secured to forward part of saddle so that the gun barrel rests beneath the "fenders."

saddle galls: Sores on the back of a horse caused by chafing of a saddle. A top hand "airs" his saddle frequently and keeps his saddle blankets clean to avoid galls.

saddle pounder: A rider.

saddle tramp: A wandering, drifting cowboy. Similar to a hobo. See *grubline rider: chuckline rider.*

saddle tree: The wooden frame of a saddle, hence the expression, "deep in the wood," signifying the inability of horse to throw rider. There are many different designs of saddle trees and each is important as regards stability and value. Saddle builders adopt a popular tree and specialize in that particular one, the Robinson being a well-known "tree" in the Southwest.

sage brush: A small-leaved shrub growing in arid sections of Southwest. See *black chapparal.*

sage hen: A woman; girl; filly; heifer.

sagging belt: A belt heavily loaded with guns, cartridges and holsters.

saguaro: The giant Arizona cactus, growing to 60 feet in height.

salivate: To shoot anyone.

salt grass: An arid country grass. Sand grass. Basket grass.

salt lick: Salt placed out on the range for cattle. May be a natural salt outcropping. See *alkali lick.*

salty: Tough; mean; full of fight and fire; refers to bad horses or men. See *curly worlf: rough: snuffy.*

salty oxen: Wild steers. See *wild ladinos.*

sashay: To walk or go. Also, a dance term.

savena: A horse.

savvied the cow: Understood the cattle business.

savvy: Understand? Misspelling of Spanish word *sabe.* To savvy anything means something more than a simple understanding. It implies a thorough knowledge of the subject.

saw-bones: A doctor. See *pill roller.*

sawed-off: A shotgun with shortened barrels. Usually loaded with buckshot, nine to the shell. See *scattergun.*

scads: Plenty; a quantity. See *Hell's slew and slather.*

Scalded back: Said of a horse's back which has had the skin rubbed off by action of saddle. See *saddle galls.*

scatterbrained: Thoughtless; reckless; not dependable.

scatter gun: A shotgun. Very effective at short range. See *sawed-off.*

scratch: To spur a horse; to reef or rake him. See *comb* and *rowel.* To curry him out.

screwbean: A mesquite bush. Spanish tornillo.

screwing down tight in saddle: Sitting tight with spurs locked into cinch to avoid being thrown from horse.

screwed on tight: A saddle which has had cinches well tightened before the bronc is forked. If the cinches are loose, the rider may get piled in dirt by a flopping saddle.

screw worms: Maggot-like worms infesting cuts and open sores on a critter. Very hard to get rid of.

see can you: Try and see if you can.

seeing daylight: The light which shines between the rider of a bronc and the saddle seat. *Usually* foretells a bad spill. Also referred to as "sloppy riding."

seguro Miguel!: Sure, Mike! Spanish term adopted in Southwest.

selling a brand: This includes the sale of all stock which have been marked with that particular brand.

Señor: Mister; sir. Spanish.

Señóra: Madam; mistress. Spanish.

señorita: Miss. Spanish.

serape: A narrow shawl worn over shoulder. Spanish.

set on his tail: A horse braced back on his haunches ready to jump.

set the hair on him: To ride a horse until he quits fighting. See *rode his horse to a standstill.*

setting on their heels: Haunched down. See *hunker.*

seven-up: A card game comprising "high, low, jick, jack and game."

shack: A crude house; shanty; jacal. See *dugout.* The term "shack" is also applied to the stagecoach.

shadow-rider: One who while riding looks at and admires his shadow and finds it good.

shakedown: A bed on the ground or floor; a pallet. See *hot roll.*

shake his gun loose: To prepare for action.

shaps: Same as *chaps.*

sharp's carbine: A rifle.

shebang: The ranch as a whole; see *outfit* and *spread.*

sheep wagon: The living quarters of the sheep herder. The wagon is canvas-covered and is provided with a bunk, stove, etc. It is moved from place to place with the grazing blatters.

sher'f: Sheriff.

shindig: Cowboy term for dance, celebration or fiesta.

shootin' iron: A six-gun. See *gun.*

shorthorn: A newcomer; tenderfoot; greenhorn. See *pilgrim.* It also refers to a breed of cattle. The man from places other than Texas is sometimes called a shorthorn.

short shrift: Quick work.

shovin': Driving, herding or pushing cattle while on trail. In some sections it refers to circling the herd preparatory to halting for the night. See *bed-down* and *working cattle.*

shuck: To throw away; cast off. Also, a cigarette rolled in a corn husk; the covering of a Mexican hot tamale. A Mexican is sometimes called a "shuck."

shut-eye: Sleep.

sí: Yes. Spanish.

side-lined him: The act of hobbling a horse's front foot to the hind foot on the same side to prevent straying. A three-foot length of rope is used in the side-lining.

side me: Ride along with me; accompany me.

sidewinder: The desert rattlesnake, so named on account of its peculiar side motion when crawling. As applied to a man, the term expresses meanness or treachery.

siesta: The afternoon nap. Spanish.

sign camp: Camps which are occasionally established on the outskirts of an entire range. There are usually two men to each camp whose duty it is to herd back all cattle which may have drifted across the line. The man who rides the sign camp range line is call a line rider.

sinkers: Biscuits. See *doughgods* and *terrapin.*

sink of iniquity: Cowboy term for a saloon or brothel.

six-gun: A six-shooter. See *gun.*

six-shooterful: Handy with guns. See *gun slick* and *gun hawk.*

size up: To examine anything carefully; estimate possibilities.

skeed-up: Drunk; having partaken of too much skee, or whiskey. see *geed-up.*

skewbald: Piebald; a horse splashed with different colors. See *paint horse* and *pinto.*

skin full: Drunk. See *skeed-up* and *tanked.*

skinned out: Left in a hurry. Also refers to a beef carcass after the hide has been removed. See *skinner.*

skinner: The driver of horse or mule teams. A mule skinner. See *bull whacker.* Also, the cowboy whose duty it is to remove the hide from dead critter. See "stiff-man."

skullduggery: Foul doings; misdeeds; underhand business.

skunk: See *polecat.*

sky pilot: A preacher; minister.

slant a gun: To point or aim a gun.

slant ear: The slant of a bronc's ears usually skews his goodness or meanness.

slapped in the face with a spade: Buried.

slather: A whole slew; a lot; plenty; a huge quantity.

sleeper: A critter that is earmarked but not branded; a lightly branded calf; a calf with brand obliterated.

slick: An unbranded cow.

slick-ear: An animal with unmarked ears; not earmarked.

slicker: An oilskin or waterproofed coat, usually long and loose. Called "fish" or "oilskin." See *fish.*

slicker roll: The slicker rolled tightly and lashed between rider and saddle horn. Serves same purpose as bucking-roll.

slicker pack: Personal belongings rolled into slicker and usually lashed behind saddle cantle.

slick foxin': Doing clever tricks; pulling a ruse.

slick-up: To don your best bib and tucker; puttin' on your "store" clothes.

slog: To walk with a careless, slip-shod or awkward gait.

slope: To go away; to depart. See *light a shuck.*

sloppy: Careless or loose riding.

slow elk: Prime steer belonging to a neighboring outfit, killed for beef. To slow elk a steer is to surreptitiously kill it.

slow elk vs company beef: Slow elk (a prime, fat steer) always tastes better than company beef, due to its belonging to another outfit. The company beef might be a cull; the slow elk, never.

slug: A bullet of a heavy calibre.

smack dab: Dead center; a bull's eye; directly into. "We ran smack dab into th' sher'f."

smear: To throw or pile up.

smoke out: To drive from concealment or hiding.

smoke-pole: Smoke-wagon; a six-shooter. See Gun.

smoke-tree: A small tree or shrub growing to twelve feet, common in arroyos. The indigo bush. The tree bears cluster of small flowers which give it a smoky appearance and is covered with grey, spiny twigs.

smoothie: An old horse with worn down teeth; also, a clever person.

shag: To successfully rope a critter. See *snare.*

snake: An odious person. As verb: to drag anything.

snake remedy: Whiskey; panther sweat; red-eye. See *pizen.*

snapper: A breaker of wild horses. See *bronc buster.*

snapping broncs: Teaching broncs the use of saddle and bridle. "The peelers were busy snapping out a bunch of broncs."

snap team: An extra team hitched to wagon tongue to assist in pulling wagon from mudhole or quicksand. A "snatch" team.

snare: To rope an animal; to trap. See *dab: snag.*

snoozer: A derisive term applied to sheepman.

snortin' pole: Snubbing pole in corral.

snubbing post: A deeply imbedded timber, some five feet above ground, set firmly to withstand shock of snubbed horses when fighting the rope.

snuffy: Treacherous; wild; a horse anxious to buck or run, as a "snuffy bronc." See *boogery: spooky.*

snuffy steers: Wild steers, hard to handle. See *wild ladings: salty oxen.*

soap 'er up: Add fancy details; embellish. See *tale tales.*

soaked: Drunk. See *skeed: tanked.*

soap-weed: A small tree or brush growing in Southwest.

sod buster: A dirt farmer. See *fool hoe man: nester: squatter: cornfed granger: churn twister.*

soft soap: Blarney; guff; hooey. See *bushwah.*

sold his saddle: Synonymous to pawning the family jewels. When a cowpoke sells his saddle, he has reached the bottom of his pile.

solo: A card game. See *seven-up: monte: stud.*

sombrero: A wide-brimmed hat worn in Southwestern states. See *lid: J.B.: Stetson.*

some'r's: Somewhere.

son-of-a-gun or **son-of-a-gun-in-a-sack:** A cow camp delicacy very much like meat pie. Made from sweetbreads and other choice parts of the beef; a Johnny-in-a-sack.

Sonora longhorns: Ancestors of the Texas longhorns. Wild Mexican cattle.

Sooners: A term applied to homesteaders who sneaked through the guard of soldiers along the territorial lines of Oklahoma before the signal was given for the big run in 1889. Oklahoma is now known as the "Sooner State."

soogans: Bedding; blankets; heavy comforts. See *bed roll: hot roll: shakedown.* Also spelled "soggans."

so's: So as.

sotol: A beverage distilled from fermented cactus sap. Used mainly in Mexico and along the border. Has an innocent taste but if very potent. See *tequila.*

sound as a quarter hoss: Without flaws; intact.

sourdough: A bachelor: A cook; the dough from which the camp cook makes his biscuits. In the plural denotes the biscuits themselves.

sourdough crock: The mixing bowl for biscuit dough. To wash it out is to ruin it.

sow belly: Sow bosom: Bacon; salt pork.

spade bit: A bit with a flat piece of steel fastened to the bar. This flat piece being inside the horse's mouth is a very cruel contraption when improperly used, so is also called a "stomach pump." See **bit** and **bridle bit.**

Spanish bayonet: The common yucca of the Southwest. Quijote in Spanish.

Spanish bit: Same as *spade bit.*

Spanish dagger: The *Spanish bayonet.*

spavin: A boney swelling on horses' hock due to inflammation.

spilled: Thrown from a horse or steer. See *chewed dirt.*

spilled his guts: Told all he knew, withholding nothing.

spinner: A bucking horse which whirls backward instead of forward. Very confusing to rider.

spirits of co'n likker: Very potent whiskey. See *pizen.*

split: an ear mark made by splitting the ear. See *overbit: underbit: steeple fork.*

spoiled horse: A horse which was improperly handled at the time of breaking; a man-made outlaw.

spook: The frighten or scare.

spooky: Nervous; easily frightened. *Boogery.*

Spoon vittles: Fancy eats; more particularly, food which should be eaten with aid of knife, fork and spoon instead of *lunch hooks.*

spread: A ranch, large or small. The cow outfit as a whole. See *outfit.*

sprouty: Touch; truculent; easily offended. See *get their hackles up* and *on the prod.*

spur: The badge of cowboy knighthood. See *rake: comb: rowel.* To "curry him out."

spur chains: The chain fitting under the instep of boot to assist in holding spur in position.

spur leather: A strap fitting snugly over instep for the same purpose as *spur chain.*

spurs: As much a part of the cowboy's outfit as his saddle. They not only assist the rider in guiding and controlling his horse but also help him in retaining his seat. In surcingle riding when spur rowels are locked or taped, they may be "hooked" into the band to prevent rider from being thrown. See **locked spurs.**

squared away: Smooth going; no remaining obstructions.

squat: To take possession of a plot of land; the land or claim itself. See *nester.* Also to sit on the hams. See *hunker.*

squatter: One who takes possession of a plot of land without having title to same. Very unpopular with cowmen.

squaw: An Indian woman whether young or old. Opposite of *buck.*

squaw-hitch: A hitch for holding packs in place. "Their beds 'squaw-hitched' on a pack mule." Also called "Mormon-tangle."

squawman: Any man, other than an Indian, who marries or lives with an Indian squaw.

squaw ranch: A ranch owned or operated by a woman.

squaw winter: An early snow or bad weather preceding an Indian summer.

squinch-eyed: Squint-eyed; cross-eyed.

squirt: A young fellow; yonker; younker; yunker; young'un; stripling; boy; kid; frying-size. See *button.*

squeezer: A narrow chute into which cattle are driven and branded standing up; a snappin' turtle.

stack-up: The condition or ability of anything or anybody. "How yu' stackin'-up?"

stage coach: A horse drawn vehicle used in conveying passengers, baggage and express from one point to another. See *shack.*

stake: To furnish money, supplies or equipment. See *grubstake.* A "small stake" is a small amount of property or money.

stake and rider fence: A fence built of poles and braced with other poles.

stake pin: An iron or wooden peg to which a picket rope is tied, allowing horses to graze the length of the rope but prevents them from straying; a picket pin.

stallion: A male horse which has not been castrated.

stamp brand: The conventional branding iron mark.

stampede: The wild, uncontrolled rush of cattle or horses away from the herd proper. A fearsome thing in the cattle country. Also said of humans when they rush to a new mining location. Another name for *rodeo: round-up* or "celebration."

stamp iron: The "made" branding iron. See *stamp brand.*

stand hitched: To stay in one spot. "The well-trained horse would stand hitched all day although he was only 'tied loose' with dangling reins."

steeple fork: An earmark cut on cattle by slicing a small niche out of ear. See *overbit: underbit: split.*

steer: The young male of the cattle which has been castrated.

steer buster: A cowpoke who rides wild steers at a rodeo. Due to the shape of body and looseness of skin, steers are not easy to ride.

steer roping: The art of roping, throwing and tying the feet of a wild steer, single-handed. This is one of the events of a rodeo celebration but is also part of cowboy's duties during round-up.

stepped aboard: Mounted a horse; hit leather; climbed aboard; straddled. See *forked.*

Stetson: A popular brand of headgear, sometimes running into important money. See *J.B.; lid; sombrero; XXXX Beaver.*

stewball: A corruption of *skewbald,* which see.

stick and mud chimney: A fireplace chimney built of sticks, heavily plastered with mud.

stiff: A corpse; dead 'un; also used to express "dead drunk." See *skeed-up: tanked.*

stiff man: The man, usually an old or crippled cowboy, whose duty it is to drive around the range and burn or bury the carcasses of dead stock.

stinker: Something small or mean; a clever child; also used in referring to an odious person.

stinkweed: The *jimson* weed.

stirrups: The wood, metal or leather foot rests of the saddle which assist the rider in mounting, retaining his seat, and easing his weight when in the saddle.

stirrup leathers: The straps running from the saddle tree and upon which the stirrups are hung. They are covered by the "fenders."

stock detective: A man employed by a Cattlemen's Association to ferret out any mysteries relating to rustled stock of members or any finagling as to the brands.

stock horse: A colt or mare used for breeding.

stockinged: A horse with lower legs a different color from that of body, usually white. "He forked the stocking-footed nag."

stomach pump: A spade bit.

stomp dance: A "stamp" dance. Sometimes western dances are referred to as "stomp dances." A Stomp Dance is also a tribal dance of the Apache Indians.

straddled leather: Mounted a horse. See *stepped aboard: forked.*

stray: A horse or cow brute that wanders to outside ranges. The *stray man* is the cowboy whose duty it is to return these strays to the home range by representing his employer at round-ups on foreign ranges. See *Rep.*

stretch: To rope and throw a critter for branding.

stretch a lariat: To hang. See *String-up: Necktie party: Cottonwood fruit.*

stretch the blanket: To tell lies. See *Tall Tale.* Blankets are sometimes stretched when there is a crap game, black-jack, stud or draw-poker in operation.

string: The cowboy's working horses. The lariat is also referred to as "string," "twine." See *Hemp.* Strings may be *hoggin' strings* or *piggin' strings* or the rawhide thongs which hold saddle leather in place but which are sometimes used to tie packages to saddle.

string along: To follow.

strings tied to it: A proposition with many angles or complications.

string-up: To hang a man. See *cottonwood fruit: necktie party: stretch a lariat.*

stud: Same as *stallion.* Also, a card game, the abbreviation of stud poker. See *black jack: solo; monte; seven-up.*

Studebaker: A popular brand of wagon.

sucker: A horse which sucks wind while biting something.

suggan: Blanket or bedroll. See *hit roll: soogan.*

sun dodger: A lazy, shiftless gent.

sun fish: The back-breaking movement of a horse when bucking. The body is curved, the horse jumps stiff-legged, sideways. Very effective in dislodging a rider.

sunset rowel: A multi-spiked spur wheel. See *rowel.*

surcingle: A belt or girth, made of webbing, hair or leather, which is buckled around a critter's belly. The surcingle has no stirrups and is used in riding the Brahma bull, horses and steers. See *ride slick: spurs: and locked spurs.*

suspenders: A cowboy has no more use for suspenders than he would for a coat, canteen or noon lunch on a day's ride.

swag: Loot; a thief's booty; boodle. Also, a sag, swale or draw.

swallow-fork: To travel carelessly. Also, an earmark resembling a forked-notch or swallow. See *over-bit: under-bit: split: steeple fork.*

swamper: A cleaner of stables; a flunky or helper in saloon or cook's quarters; an assistant on a freighter's wagon or on a 20-horse or mule team outfit. See *bull cook.*

swap: To trade or exchange anything.

swap ends: Applied to a horse that jumps high and whirls while in mid-air.

swear words: The cowpuncher's lurid vocabulary of dignified and high-faluting cuss words is truly amazing.

sweatin' a stretch: Working on ranch during dull months for grub only.

sweeled: Peeved. See *on the prod.* "Must be swelled 'bout something we said."

swing a wide loop: To steal horses or rustle cattle: also, to be carefree; free of restraint.

swing brand: A letter, figure or symbol hanging from an inverted quarter circle, known as Swing R, Swing K, etc.

Swing into leather: Hit the saddle. See *forked: straddled leather.*

Swing riders: The flank riders of a moving herd who travel midway between *point riders* and *drag riders.*

swivel duke: The gentleman who rides the swivel chair in an office; a loafer; a gaudily dressed hombre.

-T-

tail: To follow or bring up the rear. See *drag rider.*

tail, hide and beller: The whole works; all there is.

tailing: Dumping a critter head over heels, while traveling at a good gait, by simply grabbing its tail and twisting it to one side. This spill so stuns the *bunch quitter* that he is usually willing to be a good boy the rest of the day.

tail-up: To seize the tail of a bogged animal and assist it from mud hole or quicksand. Very interesting, especially if mud is deep and half-frozen. In "Chinook-wind" countries the unexpected warmth often gets cattle down and they must then be "tailed-up" or left to freeze to death when the next cold snap hits them. See *Chinook.*

tail-rider: A *drag-rider.* Men who ride at the rear of a moving herd.

take out through: Go through; go across.

take the big leap: To die; shuffle off. See *cash-in.*

talk turkey: Talk seriously; right to the point.

talky-talk: A confab. See *pow-wow: wau-wau: palaver.*

tallow: Fat on a critter. "Lost some tallow" means lost weight.

tall, rough, uncut: The wild places; the open spaces.

tall tale: A flight of the imagination; a Baron Munchausen. Very popular among cowboys in bunkhouses at night. A story of the *Pecos Bill* or Paul Bunyan type. See *windy.*

tally: A count of the stock; also, the total count itself.

tally book or sheet: The book in which a record of the tally or count is kept.

tally man: The cowboy who keeps tab of the newly branded calves at the spring round-up.

tangled mitts: Shook hands.

tank: A pond or small body or water; a reservoir of wood, metal, mud or concrete construction.

tanked: Drunk; shot full of sotol or teed-up on tequila. See *skeed-up.*

tanking-up: Drinking. See *manager* and *millin' around a jug.*

tapadero: The tee-fender which covers the front end of a stirrup. Abbreviated to "tap." In Spanish means a large stopper.

taped spurs: Locked rowels for rodeo work.

tarantula juice: Whiskey; tornado juice. See *pizen: sotol: tequila: snake remedy: likker: bug juice.*

tarpaulin or tarp: A square of waterproofed canvas very useful in the cow country. The cowpoke uses the *tarp* to roll his *suggan* in before *squaw-hitching* it to his *pack horse.*

tassejo: Jerked beef. Spanish.

teguas: Cowhide moccasins. Sp.

Tejano: A Texan. See *Longhorn* and *Texican.*

telling off the riders: Said of the foreman when he issues instructions to the various riders for the day's work.

tenderfoot: A newcomer; greenhorn; greener. See *pilgrim.* One unaccustomed to range life and methods. A jigger who might wear his spurs upside-down or be unable to drink from a stream because he didn't have a tin cup. The butt of countless jokes.

tepee: An Indian dwelling built of poles and covered with skins or canvas. Also a small tent in which to sleep while away from the main ranch.

tequila: A powerful Mexican beverage. Give a horned toad a swig of tequila and he'll spit in an alligator's face. See *sotol* and *pulque.*

Terrapin: A species of dry-land turtle, relished as food by the prairie Indian. The word also has a certain sinister reference to sourdough biscuits as made by some cooks.

Texican: A native of Texas. See *Longhorn* and *Tejano.*

the'd: There would be.

thimbleheel: The small, high heels of a cowpuncher's boots. On account of the sharp, forward slant of these high heels, walking is somewhat difficult and extremely awkward.

think tank: The head - which sometimes contains a brain.

this-a-way: This way; in this manner.

thongs: Strips of rawhide or leather, used for tying and lacing.

thorns: The Great Southwest is spiked with cactus spines and thorny bushes. Among some of the popular brands we find the cat-claw, wild century-plant, desert holly, hedgehog cactus, saguaro or giant cactus, barrel cactus, fish-hook cactus, cholla, prickly pear, devil's claw, deer-horn cactus, Spanish dagger, white-thorn, manzanita, and the chapparals. These are but a few of the thousand and one versions of cacti and thorny brushes which give the cowpoke a valid alibi for his use of the picturesque *batwing chaps.*

throw down on: To cover another person with a gun. *See get the drop.*

thumb-buster: The old style, single-action pistol which required cocking with the thumb each time it was fired. See *gun: fanning.*

tie: To fasten. See *ground tied.* A trained horse never strays when "ground tied" or tied "loose," that is, with the reins trailed to the ground.

tie-hard: Said of a lariat when the end is tied fast to saddle horn to aid in holding a roped critter. See *dally.* The *rope* or *whale line* is invariably tied to the saddle horn while the sixty-foot reata or *riata* is usually dallied or "snubbed."

tigers of the desert: A term formerly applied to the fierce Apache Indians.

tin cow: Canned milk; embalmed cow. See *canned cow: airtights.*

tin-horn: A pretender; fourflusher; cheat; sharper; cheap gambler. There were usually a bunch of *tin-horns* infesting the cow town gambling houses and *honkys,* ready to take the 'puncher for his summer wages.

tipping: Sawing or nipping the tip of a critter's horns so it would be unable to injure a horse.

ti-wah: Comanche Indian word meaning "white man."

toe the line: Holster your gun!: follow the straight and narrow; watch your step; 'tend to your own biz: be careful of conduct.

tol'able: Tolerable; passable, fair to middlin'; moderately good.

tomahawk: Cowboy word for a hatchet; weapon used by Indians.

tonchi bola: A Choctaw Indian food, prepared by cooking hominy and meat together.

took bit in teeth: Ran away. When a bad horse manages to work bridle bit between his teeth he is out of control and a bucking contest or runaway results. Also refers to impulsive action of a person. See *cold jawed.*

top hand: An expert cowhand, fully qualified to handle any of the various cow country duties. The *point rider* is always a top hand; an expert *cutter* is a top horse. There are top ropers, top riders, etc., "top" signifying "best."

top off: The first daily ride of a bucking horse. "After the broncs were 'topped off' we settled for a long ride."

top screw: The ranch foreman; straw boss. See *boss.*

tortilla: Mexican bread; a thin cake, rolled by hand and browned on top of stove. Prepared from a mixture of flour, cornmeal, water and milk; an omelet; pancake. See *rawhide flapjacks.*

to'rd: Toward.

tote: To carry anything; *totin':* Carrying. "That hombre totes twin six-guns."

tough as Spanish beef: Plenty tough. See *salty.*

trail: To follow or track an animal or person. See *cut his sign.* The art of following "sign" was a useful and necessary requirement of the oldtimer. A *trail* is also a cow country thoroughfare.

trail a flying bird: The man who seemed to have this sixth sense was rated an expert tracker or "sign" reader.

trail boss: The man in charge of a moving cattle herd.

trail brand: The temporary brand placed upon critters just before they were moved. The brand was proof of ownership in a strange country.

trail herd: A herd of cattle on the trail.

trail hog: A gent or outfit monopolizing the lion's share of a trail and water holes. Same as a road hog.

traipse: To walk or ride about in an aimless manner; to fool about.

travels lonesome: One who travels alone; a lone wolf.

tree: The wooden frame of a saddle. See *saddle: saddle tree.* The saddle is sometimes referred to as a "tree."

trigger: To shoot; to jerk or squeeze the trigger of a gun.

trim his wick: To administer a licking to a gent; to take a man's measure; to "trim him up."

tropa: A troop. Spanish.

truck: Dealings; business; association. "I don't want no *truck* with that *hombre*."

tunk: To strike; hit. "He tunked the critter 'atween th' horns."

twister: A bronc rider or breaker; a bronc twister. See *man.* Also, a term applied to the cyclonic winds so common on the plains.

-U-

uncork: When a horse commences to buck, he "uncorks." When a *buster* "uncorks" a horse he rides him down and takes the rough off him. See *boil over: bogged his head: onwind.*

underbit: An ear mark. See *overbit: steeple fork: split.*

unhobble his gun triggers: Shake out his guns and get them ready for action.

Unlimbered his gun: Drew his six-shooter.

unroughing a spooky bronc: Taking the rough edges off a wild, nervous horse; teaching him the use of saddle, bridle, spurs, quirt and man.

un-wax them ears: Listen carefully!; Pay attention!: Attender.

unwind: To commence bucking. See *bogged his head: onwind: uncork.*

unwind a loop: To shake out a loop in a lariat. See *build a loop.*

upped: Proceeded; want; as "upped and got hung." Also used as a poker term signifying a raise in the bet. "Pedro shoved in five bucks and I *upped* him ten."

up to scratch: Worth; up to par.

usta: Contraction of "used to."

Usted: You. Spanish. (Contraction of vuestra merced.)

-V-

vaca: A cow; beef. Spanish.

vamoose: Go!; hike; git; scat. Spanish term adopted in Southwest.

vaquero: A cowboy; herder of cows; Spanish.

vent: To "vent a brand" is to add a mark or duplicate of brand on to the original brand to indicate that the critter has traded hands.

verde: Green. Spanish.

vino: Wine. Spanish.

vinegaroon: A salty gentleman. Also, a species of scorpion. This desert beastie was once supposed to be poisonous and gets its name from the vinegar smell it emits when disturbed.

viva!: Hurrah! Spanish.

voucher: An Indian scalp. Also, the cowboy's pay check.

-W-

waddy: A cowpuncher. See *man.* There was a time when the word "waddy" referred solely to a cattle rustler.

wagon: When mules or horses are used to pack supplies, they are sometimes called *wagons.* Also see *Studebaker.*

wagon boss: The foreman or man in charge of a round-up. Also the boss over a wagon train.

walking like a hog on a rail: A staggering, awkward gait.

wall-eyed: Wide, rolling eyes; eyes of a grey or whitish cast. Horses with this type of eye are usually vicious. As applied to man, "He's a wall-eyed liar."

wall-eyed-wild: A wild critter. See *snuffy: salty oxen: wild ladings.*

waller in tallow: Wallow in fat; live a life of ease; be affluent.

wa'n't: Contraction of "was not."

war bag: Container of cowboy's personal belongings.

war bonnet: Hat; the feathered head-dress worn by Indians during tribal ceremonies. See *sombrero: rodeo.*

war paint: make-up; finery. The gals of the *honkatonk* district smeared on plenty "war paint" when the 'punchers hit town. Also refers to anger; ire. See *on the prod.*

wart hog: An old man; a scissorbill; an oldster. See *ancient.*

water hole: A spring; pond; tank; lake; dam.

wau-wau: Talk; a conference. See *talky-talk: confab: palaver: making medicine.*

weaner: A calf; more particularly, a weaned calf old enough to ship.

wedger: An uninvited person.

welch: To back down; to draw in one's horns. A *welsher* is one who cheats at a horse race.

wenta 'cootin': Went hurriedly; lost no time; breezed through like a Hades' hurricane.

wet stock: Stolen livestock. This term originated from the practice of stealing cattle on one side of the Mexican border and swimming them across the Rio Grande River to the other side.

wet stuff: Cows with calves. See *mammy* and dry *stuff.*

whack: Condition of anything: "Out of whack" means out or order. Also means to hit or strike.

whack a joke: Tell a joke.

whacker: A big lie or big liar. See *windy: tall tales.*

whale line: The lariat. The whale line is usually a "tie" line, that is, the rope is slipped through the fork in the saddle and tied to the horn.

whang: Rawhide; untanned leather; green leather; a rawhide thong.

wheeler: The wheel horse, or one of the horses nearest the wheels of a multi-team outfit, as opposed to the leader or forward horse. This applies to 20-horse or mule team outfits.

wheeling: Dragging the spur rowels on the floor as a sign of willingness to play or scrap.

whelpin' time: Springtime.

whey belly: A barrel-like paunch. See *potbelly; dough belly.*

whip socket: The receptacle for the butt of the buggy-whip.

white faces: Hereford cattle; "open-faced" cattle.

whizzer: A bluff; trick; deception.

whop dollager: Anything of a huge size; a whopper; especially applied to a *tall tale.*

whooped an' fanned: Yelled and whipped his hat.

whyn't: Contraction of "why not."

wicky: Contraction of "wicky-up." A rudely constructed Indian hut used by the Apaches, built of small limbs or long brush. Differs from the *tepee* or *wigwam,* which see.

wide loop: Refers to rustling cattle or stealing horses. "He throws a wide loop," careless as to whose cattle the loop falls on. See *long rope artist* and *swing a wide loop.*

wigwam: A cone-shaped Indian hut made of poles covered with skins or canvas. See *tepee* and *wicky.* Some 'punchers refer to any dwelling as a wigwam.

wild bunch: A band of mustangs or wild horses; a group of lawless men; *owlhooters.*

wildcat: A sheep-lined, close fitting leather jacket often used in winter by northern cowboys.

wild catch: A batch of mustangs just driven into a wild horse trap; also has reference to the stealing of cattle.

wild century plant: The agave, maguey or mescal plant. Has huge leaves with spines on the edges and a thorn at the apex. The maguey *lariat* rope comes from this plant as also does the fermented Mexican *pulque* and the distilled *mescal.* The plant was formerly thought to bloom but once in a century.

wild ladings: Wild steers. See *salty oxen: Sonora Longhorn.*

wimmin: Women. See *sage hen.*

Winchester law: To rule by might of a Winchester rifle. Very effective in settling arguments.

wind-bellied maverick: An unbranded, pot-gutted critter.

winded: To get scent of on account of the wind blowing from man to animal. "The mustangs winded me before I could shake out a loop."

windies: Wild cattle (*salty steers*) driven from brakes and badlands to open range are usually so wily, fast and contrary that they "tucker" themselves as well as the cowpokes and their horses by the time they are fairly out: hence the name.

wind-up: To get ready to buck; to *uncork.* Also to finish or complete anything.

windy: A bald-faced lie. See *tall tale: whop dollager.*

wipe 'er clean: Pay all bets; settle everything; square accounts.

with natural leaf t'baccer in his jeans: Affluent; in the money. See *waller in tallow.*

wo-haw: Comanche Indian word meaning meat or beef.

Wood: A saddle. See *deep in the wood: saddle: saddle tree: tree.*

wooden clothes: wooden kimono: Wooden overcoat: A coffin.

woolies: Sheep; Baa-a-ahs.

wooly: Tough; mean; ornery. See *salty: curly wolf: on the prod: snuffy.*

wooshers: Hogs; churn twister's delight; hoe man's hobby; rooters.

wop: A wuthless peson.

working cattle: Doing any of the thousand-and-one things in a cow country or on a cattle ranch which might be necessary to ensure the success of the outfit. "In California and parts of Arizona where cattle are 'worked' in the corral instead of in the open this 'working' would include the cutting out, sorting and branding." Mrs. Rak speaks to the point when she says that instead of the cowboys "working" the cattle, the cattle often "work" the cowboys.

wrangle: To herd or lead anything. To wrangle horses; to wrangle a meal. The *horse wrangler* is the cowboy who herds the remuda. The *grub wrangler* is the cook. See *dude wrangler.* A cow will not "wrangle." She must be herded or '"punched."

wrasslin': Wrestling. See *horsing around: foofarawing.*

wrinkle his back: To start bucking. See *boil over* and *uncork.* Also said of a man showing his willingness to fight. See *wheeling.*

wrinkles on his horns: This refers to man or critter as he gets older and wiser. See *moss head* or *moss horn.*

-X-

xxxx: Four x. A brand of beaver hat. See *J.B.: sombrero* and *lid.*

-Y-

yack: A stupid hombre; a dummy.

yahoo: Same as *yack.*

yamp: To steal; rustle; swipe.

yarn: To swap talk. To tell *tall tales* or *windys.*

yawp: To whine; fuss; complain. "The real cowboy never whines." As noun, means mouth or trap. "Shet yore yawp."

y'ask: Contraction of "you ask."

yearling: One year old. See *prime long twos.*

yellow from collar to crupper: Th extreme of cowardice.

yipe: Same as *yawp.*

yippee!: The cowboy's exuberant yell.

yore: Your.

yore sights are set too high: You are looking too far ahead.

yo's: Yours.

you-all: Southwest colloquialism.

you better drag it: A suggestion to leave. See *vamoose.*

young sprout: Young squirt: A young person. See *button: younker: frying size.*

younker: A young fellow. See *button.*

you-uns: Refers to several persons. See *you-all.*

yucca: A Southwest desert plant. Beautiful when in bloom. See *Spanish bayonet.*

yucca country: The desert and desert's edge; the arid country.

-Z-

zapatos: Shoes. Spanish.

zipper: A fast bucker; a cowboy with an oversupply of "wim, wigor and witality." "He's a zipper, awright."

zorra: A fox; a strumpet. Spanish.

zurron: A sheepherder's pouch. Spanish.

www.ingramcontent.com/pod-product-compliance
Lightning Source LLC
LaVergne TN
LVHW090957080826
845145LV00003B/1038

* 9 7 8 1 9 6 4 0 9 4 0 7 6 *